NEBRASKA

NEBRASKA BY ROAD

NATIONAL FOREST & GRASSLAND

MILES

0 20 40 60 80 100

Sioux City South

Bellevue

Nebraska City

Falls City

Missouri R.

Fremont

Omaha

Lincoln

Beatrice

Fairbury

Missouri R.

Logan Cr.

Norfolk

Columbus

Big Blue R.

Crete

York

Grand Island

Hastings

Elkhorn R.

Platte R.

Little Blue R.

O'Neill

Cedar R.

281

Sherman Reservoir

Davis Creek Reservoir

Kearney

Holdrege

Republican R.

Niobrara R.

Missouri R.

Bassett

Calamus Reservoir

Middle Loup

North Loup

Nebraska National Forest

Gothenburg

Cozad

Harlan County Lake

Beaver Cr.

McCook

Valentine

Moon Lake

Calamus R.

South Loup

North Platte

Platte R.

Merritt Reservoir

Middle Loup

Dismal R.

Ogallala

Red Willow Cr.

Hugh Butler Lake

Republican R.

Lake C. W. McConaughy

Freedman Cr.

Enders Reservoir

Samuel R. Mackenzie National Forest

Chadron

Nebraska National Forest

Box Butte Reservoir

White R.

Niobrara R.

Northport

Sidney

Ogdala National Grassland

Lake Minatare

Scottsbluff

Kimball

North Platte R.

5,424 ft.

N E S W

CELEBRATE THE STATES
NEBRASKA

Ruth Bjorklund

BENCHMARK BOOKS

MARSHALL CAVENDISH
NEW YORK

For Rhon

Benchmark Books
Marshall Cavendish Corporation
99 White Plains Road
Tarrytown, New York 10591-9001

Copyright © 2001 by Marshall Cavendish Corporation

Library of Congress Cataloging-in-Publication Data

Bjorklund, Ruth.
Nebraska / by Ruth Bjorklund.
p.   cm. — (Celebrate the states)
Includes bibliographical references (p.) and index.
ISBN 0-7614-1311-1
1. Nebraska—Juvenile literature. [1. Nebraska.] I. Title. II. Series.
F666.3 .B58 2002
978.2—dc21 00-050808

Maps and graphics supplied by Oxford Cartographers, Oxford, England

Photo research by Ellen Barrett Dudley and Matthew J. Dudley

Photo Research by Candlepants Incorporated

Cover Photo: Joel Sartore

The photographs in this book are used by permission and through the courtesy of: *Corbis*: David Muench,
6-7, 10-11, 108; James L. Amos, 15, 98-99, 115 (left), 132; Yogi, Inc., 16 (top); Tom Bean, 18, 20;
Phil Schermeister, 19; Philip Gould, 48-49, 103, 112; Morton Beebe, 54; Annie Griffiths Belt, 55, 106;
Richard Hamilton Smith, 60, 121; Buddy Mays, 79; Bettmann, 85, 92, 94, 97, 124 (top & lower), 125 (top
& lower), 126, 127, 128, 131; Joe McDonald, 115 (center); Chase Smith, 115 (right); Jeff Vanuga, 118; Rufus
F. Folks, 129. *Joel Sartore*: 16 (bottom), 22, 23, 61, 62, 67, 69, 74, 80, 82-83, 98-99, 110, 123, back cover.
Museum of Nebraska Art, University of Nebraska at Kearney: 24-25, 27. *Nebraska State Historical Society*: 30, 34,
35, 39, 41, 44, 46, 87, 89, 95. *Scotts Bluff National Park*: 32. *Cheryl Richter*: 57, 59, 64-65, 71, 73, 77, 78.

Printed in Italy

3   5   6   4   2

CONTENTS

NEBRASKA IS . . .

Nebraska is a land of quiet beauty . . .

"I was often struck with admiration at the sight of the picturesque scenes which we enjoyed all the way up the Platte. . . . I have seen groups of islands that one might easily take, from a distance, for fleets under sail, . . . and the rapid flow of the river past them made them seem to be flying over water." —Father Pierre Jean De Smet, 1840

. . . where the earth gives up great harvests.

"There are few scenes more gratifying than a spring plowing in that country, where the furrows of a single field often lie a mile in length, and the brown earth, with such a strong, clean smell and such a power of growth and fertility in it, yields itself eagerly to the plow . . . with a soft, deep sigh of happiness."

—Author Willa Cather, *O Pioneers!*

"'We came out to Nebraska to raise popcorn,' said Jonas Jonas, 'and I guess we got nearly enough popcorn this year for the popcorn poppers and all the friends and relations of all the popcorn poppers in these United States.'" —Writer Carl Sandburg

Nebraska was settled by resilient pioneers, who built their homes from chunks of earth.

"Many fine Americans were born in such holes in the earth: Senators, oil magnates, doctors, writers, stockmen and preachers— all kinds of people." —Mari Sandoz, Sandhills author

Nebraska is beloved by many . . .

"It is beautiful only in the eyes of those who live here and in the memories of the Nebraska-born whose dwelling in far places has given them moments of home-sickness for the low rolling hills, the swell and dip of the ripening wheat, the fields of sinuously waving corn and the elusively fragrant odor of alfalfa."

—Author Bess Streeter Aldrich

. . . though not by all.

"What people on I-80 want to see is Nebraska in their rear-view mirror."   —Steve Haack, Lincoln artist

Still, it is a haven in the heartland.

"I have lived in this state my whole life, yet I never cease to be amazed by its beauty and its people. Nebraska is still the great, open land of new horizons that the Native Americans knew, and its people are still as open as those horizons."

—Former Nebraska governor Ben Nelson

Nebraska is a state of subtle glories. The earth is fruitful, and farmers harvest food for tables far beyond the nation's borders. Waters deep beneath the land's surface nourish the entire Great Plains. Hardworking citizens take immense pride in the diversity of their heritage. Cities burst with energy and enterprise. As novelist Jim Harrison fondly proclaims, it is a realm that is "divinely ordinary."

1 RIVERS AND PRAIRIES

Looming large across the middle of the continent is the state of Nebraska. Its immense landscape is full of fertile farmlands, broad prairies, jagged rocks, vast sand dunes, and racing rivers.

EASTERN NEBRASKA

Rivers abound in Nebraska. The Missouri River forms all of the eastern and part of the northern boundary of the state. The Missouri, once called the Mighty Mo, has been slowed by dams, but in a section of northeast Nebraska, it runs wild past fertile riverbanks, scenic bluffs, and woodlands.

One hundred million years ago, a great inland ocean covered parts of Nebraska. Later, as the earth warmed and the water withdrew, large salt marshes were left behind. Shorebirds such as black terns and yellowlegs still flock to the green and marshy areas of southeastern Nebraska. Eastern Nebraska, south of the Platte River, is often called Willa Cather country. A daughter of early pioneers, the author saw only a few trees alongside rivers and streams. Elsewhere, there was just an endless ocean of grass. Cather wrote, "Trees were so rare in that country . . . that we used to feel anxious about them and visit them as if they were persons." Today, towns and farms have replaced the native prairie grass. But the sound of crickets, the stunning color of wildflowers, and an

LAND AND WATER

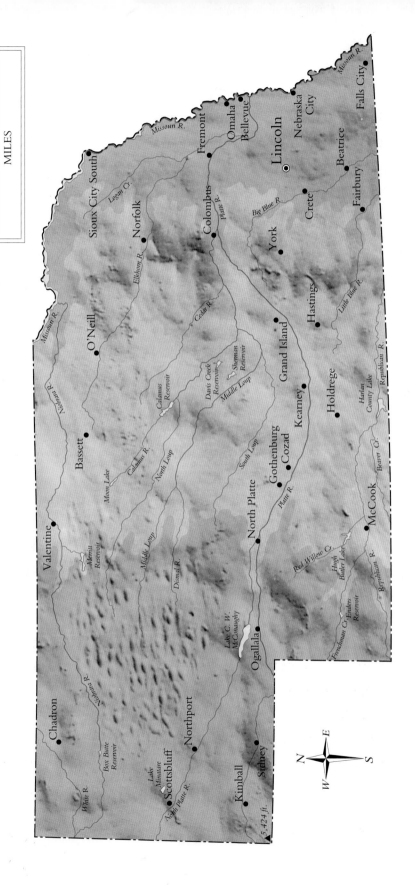

	3,000 – 6,000 ft.
	1,500 – 3,000 ft.
	600 – 1,500 ft.

MILES

0   20   40   60   80   100

Sioux City South
Norfolk
Fremont
Omaha
Bellevue
Lincoln
Nebraska City
Falls City
Beatrice
Fairbury
Crete
York
Colombus
Hastings
Grand Island
O'Neill
Kearney
Holdrege
Bassett
Gothenburg
Cozad
North Platte
McCook
Valentine
Chadron
Northport
Ogallala
Scottsbluff
Kimball
Sidney

Missouri R.
Logan Cr.
Elkhorn R.
Platte R.
Big Blue R.
Little Blue R.
Cedar R.
Niobrara R.
Calamus Reservoir
Davis Creek Reservoir
Sherman Reservoir
Middle Loup
Republican R.
Harlan County Lake
Calamus R.
North Loup
South Loup
Platte R.
Beaver Cr.
Moon Lake
Middle Loup
Dismal R.
Merritt Reservoir
Red Willow Cr.
Hugh Butler Lake
Republican R.
Frenchman Cr. Enders Reservoir
Lake C. W. McConaughy
Box Butte Reservoir
Lake Minatare
North Platte R.
White R.
Niobrara R.

5,424 ft.

N
E
W
S

occasional glimpse of the greater prairie chicken still recall the magnificent prairies that once covered the region.

CENTRAL NEBRASKA

South-central Nebraska contains the Big Bend Reach of the Platte River. French for "flat," the Platte is aptly named. It has long been described as "a mile wide, an inch deep and uphill all the way." The Platte starts high in the Rockies as two rivers, the North Platte and the South Platte. They come together in western Nebraska, flowing as one great river across the state. Dams and irrigation channels have reduced the Platte to less than half its original size everywhere but here. In this wide section, silty sandbars and wayward currents create a paradise for birds. Feeding on grubs, snails, and corn, most of the world's sandhill cranes stop by in spring to fatten up before heading to Canada and Russia to nest. Joining them are millions of geese, as well as mallard, merganser, and pintail ducks.

Across northern Nebraska runs the Niobrara River, one of the last free-flowing rivers of the Great Plains. Its river valley is exceptionally rich. Eastern and western trees merge along its banks. No farther west will you find eastern trees such as bur oak, nor any farther east will you find western ponderosa pines. A variety of creatures roam the lush region. Among them are Texas longhorn cattle, prairie dogs, white-tailed deer, and burrowing owls. Bison and elk range freely in a wildlife refuge.

Covering most of north-central Nebraska is the extraordinary region called the Sandhills. Here, the largest expanse of sand in the Western Hemisphere forms dunes as high as three hundred feet.

Sandhill cranes sometimes greet each other with a lively dance of bows and leaps.

Roots of wild grasses anchor the sand in place. Unlike other sandy areas of the world, the Sandhills are blessed with water. Nestled in the valleys between the dunes are hundreds of natural lakes and streams. One local muses, "The Sandhills' lakes may not be very deep, but they sure hold a lot of fish." Birds such as teals, loons, and the rare Clark's grebes flock to the Sandhills. Bald and golden eagles soar overhead as deer, antelope, and coyotes rove the land.

"*Prairie dogs have their place, but if they stray, they better watch out!*" warns Jeanne Goetzinger of Chadron. Tunnels and hills built by prairie dogs are a nuisance to farmers.

In the early 1900s, the elk in Nebraska were hunted until not a single one remained. Today, growing herds have wandered back to the northwestern part of the state.

In the Sandhills, the Dismal and Loup Rivers flow past the only planted forest in the national forest system. In 1892, a University of Nebraska professor started planting cedars and pines on federal land. He hoped that growing a timber supply would encourage people to settle in the Sandhills. His plan wasn't successful, but today this remarkable patch of green is a magnet for songbirds, sharp-tailed grouse, wild turkeys, and greater prairie chickens.

THE PANHANDLE

Beyond the fertile prairies, you enter the windswept Panhandle of Nebraska, a wide finger of land pointing westward. When the early pioneers first spied this land, they were amazed. In his book *The Gathering of Zion*, author Wallace Stegner describes what they saw: "They had penetrated into a new world of strange forms, strange colorings, parched air, deceptive distances: buffalo country, horned toad country, wolf country—the authentic west."

In the Panhandle, giant sandstone and siltstone buttes carved by wind, snow, and sandstorms command your attention. Towering 450 feet above the Platte River, Chimney Rock stood as a beacon for nineteenth-century pioneers traveling west. A slow-moving wagon train could look across the plains and see the spire for days before coming upon it. Nearby is the formation named Scotts Bluff. Plains tribes called it *Me-a-pa-te*, meaning "the hill that is hard to go around."

North of Scotts Bluff is the most rugged area of Nebraska, the Pine Ridge region. There, craggy white cliffs and ponderosa pines are home to bison and bighorn sheep, animals that have been rescued

The vast, windswept Sandhills are home to a diverse array of plants and animals.

from near extinction and reintroduced to this magnificent land. Also in the northern Panhandle is the Oglala grasslands, an eerie landscape of rock formations and short grasses.

Buried deep beneath central and western Nebraska is the Ogallala Aquifer. The aquifer is a gigantic pool of underground water stretching from South Dakota to Texas. This vast resource was named after the town of Ogallala, Nebraska, in 1899. The aquifer formed 10,000 to 25,000 years ago when the sand and gravel beds under the plains soaked up and stored water running off the Rocky Mountains. Inventive settlers learned early on that a pump driven by a windmill could bring the Ogallala Aquifer's life-giving water to the surface.

BLOWING HOT AND COLD

Winds from the southeast carry warm sea air from the Gulf of Mexico across the continent. Temperatures on the ground warm the

Chimney Rock was the most famous landmark on the Oregon Trail. It became a national historic site on August 9, 1956.

air even more as it moves overhead. By the time it reaches Nebraska, it's hot. Summer temperatures between ninety and one hundred degrees are very familiar to Nebraskans. In the winter, wind directions shift, and cold weather blows in from the northwest.

Not that hundred-degree days or frigid ice storms aren't newsworthy, but if you are looking for something spectacular, head

Thrifty Nebraska farmers often made their own windmills from whatever materials they had, such as hubs and axles of old wagon wheels.

for Nebraska in springtime, when the weather can be ferocious. During this unpredictable season, warm winds from the south rake across the plains as chilly winds from the north bear down. When these weather fronts clash, it can be quite a performance. Lightning, thunder, tornadoes, floods, and hail can arrive with barely a moment's notice and change a pleasant afternoon into a run-for-cover tempest. Autumn, too, varies in extremes. Heather Kreiful of Nebraska City says, "You never know what to expect. Yesterday my kids went to school in shorts. Today they have on winter coats."

BALANCING NATURE

In Nebraska tornadoes and thunderstorms are fearsome foes, and so are rivers. In 1993, the Missouri River flooded much of the Great Plains, devastating southeastern Nebraska. Dams play an important part in flood control and help farmers irrigate their fields. All the major rivers in the state, except the Niobrara, are dammed. But while the dams meet many needs, they often harm fish, birds, and other animals.

Many creatures thrive near rivers where the water flows naturally, forming slow-moving backwater pools and sloughs. Dams and man-made channels have eliminated this habitat, threatening many of the state's endangered animals, such as the whooping crane, river otter, Eskimo curlew, and American peregrine.

Farms, towns, and cities have altered Nebraska forever. Prairies have been plowed under, woodlands cut down, and wetlands drained. Some animals, such as the grizzly bear, the gray wolf, and

STORMY WEATHER

A bookseller in Lincoln muses, "Just imagine what those first Europeans thought, when they got dropped off at the end of the trail and saw a Nebraska thunderstorm coming at them!" In 1881, pioneer Emily Towell recounted,

During the night the storm broke, which had been threatening all through the day, broke in all its fury. Lightning danced across the heavens in bold like streaks of fire; the thunder rolled and crashed; the wind howled and shrieked like wild and fearful demons. Then came the rain; it rained as if it had never rained before. Would the night ever end? Yes, even the longest night must draw to a close. Day dawned, finding nearly everyone wretched and ill.

The endangered whooping crane is the tallest North American bird. You can spot it in wetlands throughout Nebraska during its yearly migration.

the ruffed grouse, could not survive the settlement of Nebraska and disappeared completely.

To help save animals and the environment, in 1992 Nebraskans voted for a state lottery. Half the lottery income goes to the Nebraska Environmental Trust. Anyone with a plan to restore a stream, plant a small forest, or recycle waste products can apply to the trust for funding. This unique method is straightforward and effective, just what you would expect from the resourceful citizens of Nebraska.

2 THE FRIENDLY EARTH

Hill, by Hal Haloun

ebraska writer Mari Sandoz described her homeland as "friendly earth for hoof and plow." Through the eons, even as the land has undergone change, people and creatures have experienced the bounty of Nebraska, proving her words timeless and true.

EARLY CIVILIZATIONS

The first humans to live in Nebraska are called Paleo-Indians. They roamed the area 10,000 to 12,000 years ago. They used stone weapons to hunt beasts that gathered around watering holes. Their prey included giant bison, ground sloths, and mammoths, fore-runners of today's elephants.

No one knows why these people and animals disappeared. What is known is that the watering holes dried up, destroying trees and other vegetation. Later, around A.D. 400 to 600, other people moved to the area from eastern forests. They hunted and made tools and pottery. Their dwellings were dug into the earth and supported by poles covered with animal skins.

Between 1200 and 1450, ancestors of some modern Nebraska tribes enjoyed a period of peace and prosperity. Although they hunted, they also established small farms, planting beans and corn. They made decorative pottery and tools of bone. They traded with distant coastal civilizations and created ornaments from seashells.

In the 1860s, frontier artist William Henry Jackson traveled the Oregon Trail painting what he saw, such as this Pawnee village.

But in the late fifteenth century, terrific dust storms and droughts drove them from the region.

By the mid-1500s, the Pawnee tribe had settled in what is now Nebraska. Their many villages hugged the banks of the Platte. The Pawnee built earth lodges constructed of poles covered with brush and packed dirt. Men hunted over a wide range. Women tended fields of corn, squash, beans, and melon and gathered wild potatoes growing near the river. In summer and autumn, the entire village set out to hunt buffalo. Taking their homes—cone-shaped tepees made of buffalo skins and poles—the Pawnee moved their belongings on large frames dragged by dogs. After the hunt, the people returned to their farms to harvest their crops and to use the buffalo for food, shelter, clothing, tools, and weapons.

ENTER THE EUROPEANS

Many believe the first Europeans in Nebraska were Spanish explorers led by Francisco Vásquez de Coronado. In 1541, they ventured across the plains searching for Quivira, a legendary city made of gold. But rather than gold, Coronado described finding "little villages, and in many of these they do not plant anything and do not have any houses except of skins and sticks, and they wander around with the cows." The cows, of course, were buffalo.

Fifty years later, the French landed in North America. For two hundred years afterward, Spanish and French explorers, fur trappers, and adventurers traversed the region.

In the eighteenth century, eastern tribes such as the Oto, Omaha, Missouri, Ponca, and Winnebago escaped their enemies by migrating into what is now Nebraska. Like the Pawnee, they were farmers who lived in earth lodges and hunted buffalo for part of the year. Wandering, nomadic tribes lived in what is now western Nebraska. Year-round, the Cheyenne, Arapaho, Comanche, and Kiowa followed buffalo herds and raided other tribes' settlements.

The arrival of the white man changed the lives of Native Americans forever. Because the plains were rich in beaver, deer, mink, and elk, the Spanish and French established trading posts along the

A PAWNEE CREATION MYTH

The Plains Indians held deep spiritual ties to nature. Black Elk, a Lakota holy man, explains, "Is not the sky a father and the earth a mother, and are not all living things with feet or wings or roots their children?" Here is a creation myth of the Pawnee:

Once long ago, all things slept underground, waiting. There were herds of buffalo, antelope, wolves, rabbits, birds, and people. Then the Buffalo Woman awoke and walked among the creatures. As she passed, people and animals opened their eyes. She touched all, even those farthest from her. Suddenly, she bowed her head, and stepped away. In her place was a blinding light. Animals rose up to follow her, first a young cow, then a buffalo, then another and another, each, for a moment, standing alone in the light. Then the people arose, old and young. They all stepped onto the green grassy earth, along the great Platte River, under a blue sky filled with birds. The buffalo scattered about the prairie, and the people moved in every direction. Together, they knew that they were meant to share this place called Earth.

Platte, Republican, Niobrara, and Missouri Rivers. There was much activity. The traders bought hides and fur from the native hunters in exchange for horses, gunpowder, sugar, and whiskey—all of which corrupted the Indian way of life. Horses and guns made the western raiding tribes even more fierce and frightening. Sugar and whiskey proved irresistible to many Native Americans. Too often, they traded their valuables—horses, artworks, garments, and blankets—for

*Chief Standing Bear,
a nineteenth-century
Ponca leader*

mere cups of sugar or cheaply made alcohol. Worse, the white newcomers brought diseases previously unknown to the Indians, which
devastated their population.

THE GROWING NATION

While Native Americans and European traders harvested the bounty of the land, foreign governments competed for its ownership. Treaties and battles shifted custody between Spain and France until 1803, when France and the United States agreed to a sale known as the Louisiana Purchase. It granted all of the land between the Mississippi River and the Rocky Mountains, from Canada to the Gulf of Mexico, to the United States. The young nation had now doubled in size.

President Thomas Jefferson was eager to explore the new lands. Within a year, he commissioned Meriwether Lewis and William Clark to lead an expedition up the Missouri River and west to the Pacific Ocean. Their mission was to map, chart, and report scientific and geographic findings and make contact with native tribes. On August 3, 1804, high on a bluff above the Missouri River, they held a council with representatives of the Oto and Missouri tribes. During the meeting, Lewis and Clark offered gifts of tobacco, roasted meat, and flour to tribal chiefs who in return gave the Americans watermelons. At this meeting, on the site now known as Council Bluff, Lewis and Clark informed the chiefs about the change in government. At that time, the chiefs had no reason to feel threatened and invited the Americans to cross their lands in peace.

Two years later, President Jefferson sent Lieutenant Zebulon Pike to the Great Plains. In his report back, Pike declared that the area was made of "barren soil, parched and dryed up for eight months in the year." Considering the report, Congress saw little value in the territory and declared it "Indian Country." Laws were passed

Fort Kearny was established along the Platte River to safeguard pioneers traveling west.

preventing most whites from settling west of the Missouri River. Only trappers, traders, soldiers, and missionaries were allowed.

THE GREAT PLATTE RIVER ROAD

Although whites could not settle in what would be Nebraska, they could travel across it. Before long, thousands traveled in wagons or on foot along what the Indians called the Holy Road, or the Platte River Road. West to the Rockies they headed, and then on to Oregon, Utah, or California. The wide, flat valley was the perfect highway. Between 1841 and 1866, 350,000 pioneers followed the Platte, making the trail very well worn. This prompted General William T. Sherman to say that it had three virtues: "It was dry, it was level and it went exactly in the right direction."

SETTLING THE TERRITORY

In 1854, Nebraska became a U.S. territory. This meant that whites could now settle the region. Businessmen started a land grab right away, creating towns almost overnight. Omaha quickly became the territory's largest city with a population around one hundred. Then in 1862, Congress passed the Homestead Act, allowing people to claim 160 acres for a ten-dollar fee. After working the land for five years, the homesteaders would own the land outright. The very first person to take advantage of the Homestead Act was a Nebraskan, Daniel Freeman, who staked his claim on January 1, 1863.

Although homesteaders were enthusiastic about the Nebraska Territory, some of its driest regions, such as the Sandhills and the Panhandle, attracted very few settlers. The land was suitable for raising livestock, but it took 20 acres of wild grass to feed one cow, so ranchers needed more than 160 acres to make a living. In 1904, the Kincaid Act was passed, giving ranchers 640 acres apiece. By 1917, all public lands had been claimed.

The Civil War between Northern free states and Southern slave states broke out during the early homesteading days. Most

Daniel Freeman of Beatrice, Nebraska, was awarded the first U.S. homestead patent.

Nebraskans were against slavery. Some helped escaped slaves make their way north to freedom by hiding them in caves, cabins, barns, and homes. This network of hiding places is known as the Underground Railroad.

After the North defeated the South in 1865, ending the Civil War, more and more Americans looked west for their future. They dreamed of a railroad that would cross the continent. To help with the enormous cost of such an undertaking, Congress gave the Union Pacific Railroad huge parcels of land along the route. In nine months, workers laid 265 miles of track across Nebraska. Boomtowns sprang up along the way.

By the time Nebraska became a state on March 1, 1867, the Union Pacific Railroad stretched from Omaha to the state's western border. To raise money, the railroads began selling off the extra land Congress had given them. They advertised, "You have only to tickle [the land] with a plow and it will laugh a harvest that will gladden your hearts." People swarmed to the new state.

Workers placed 2,640 wooden ties per mile in building the Union Pacific Railroad track across Nebraska.

THE KINKAIDERS

In an effort to attract farmers to Nebraska, Congressman Moses P. Kinkaid introduced a bill for 640-acre homesteads in western Nebraska. He was hailed for helping homesteaders settle the Sandhills.

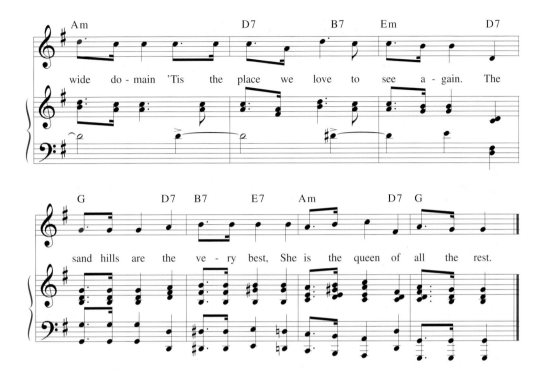

wide do-main 'Tis the place we love to see a - gain. The

sand hills are the ve - ry best, She is the queen of all the rest.

The corn we raise is our delight,
The melons, too, are out of sight.
Potatoes grown are extra fine,
And can't be beat in any clime. *Chorus*

The peaceful cows in pastures dream,
And furnish us with golden cream.
So I shall keep my Kinkaid home,
And never far away shall roam.

final chorus
Then let us all with hearts sincere,
Thank him for what he has brought us here,
And for the homestead law he made,
The noble Moses P. Kinkaid.

NO TURNING BACK

As settlers flooded into Nebraska, they displaced Native Americans. The government broke treaties with the tribes. Meanwhile, the great herds of buffalo were rapidly disappearing. The buffalo, which had given life to Native Americans, were slaughtered almost to extinction by white hunters. Without their greatest source of food and with their population weakened by disease, many Native Americans sadly gave up their ancestral homes and agreed to move onto reservations set up by the U.S. government.

Even after most of the Nebraska tribes had moved to reservations, whites disrupted their lives. In 1876, the government uprooted the Ponca tribe living on the Niobrara River and ordered them to Oklahoma. Because tribal members resisted, the government agreed to allow a party of chiefs to go in advance and judge the worthiness of the new reservation. But once the chiefs reached the new reservation, they were imprisoned. One winter night, they escaped. For fifty days, the chiefs traveled on foot, scavenging for food and sleeping unprotected on the cold ground. Once back home, they reported the harsh treatment they had received. The Ponca voted not to move, but soldiers forced them. The new reservation provided little food and no shelter. Within two years, a third of the Ponca had died. Chief Standing Bear, grieving for the loss of his son, vowed to return to Nebraska to bury the dead. After a bitter ten-week journey, Standing Bear and thirty members of his tribe reached their homeland. The chief was arrested by soldiers and brought to Fort Omaha. At his trial he told the court, "If a white man had land and someone should swindle him, that man

Railroads hired professional hunters to kill buffalo to feed workers. By 1890, white hunters had destroyed nearly every herd.

would try and get it back, and you would not blame him. Look on me. Take pity on me, and help me save the lives of the women and children."

The judge freed Standing Bear and declared, "An Indian is a person within the meaning of the law." This was the first time a white official called a Native American a person. Standing Bear was allowed to live out his life in Nebraska.

Though some tribes trusted the U.S. government, many resented losing their land. They engaged in skirmishes with white settlers. The government established outposts such as Forts Kearny, Robinson, and Atkinson to protect the settlers.

For more than ten years, western Nebraska was involved in a series of battles known as the Indian Wars. Soon after the famous battle at Little Bighorn in Montana, where in 1876, General George Custer lost to Lakota warriors under the command of Chief Crazy Horse, the U.S. Army forced thousands of Lakota to give up their weapons and move onto reservations. The next year, Crazy Horse brought two thousand of his people with him to Fort Robinson, calling for peace. There, he was assassinated. In the winter of 1878, a band of Cheyenne under Chief Dull Knife escaped an Oklahoma reservation, and dodging soldiers, trekked six hundred snowy miles to Nebraska. On January 9, 1879, they were captured near Fort Robinson. Soldiers killed most of them. Historians agree that on that night, the last Native American resistance effort had been defeated.

O PIONEERS!

For the pioneers, Nebraska was a harsh new world. In *Sandhill Sundays*, homesteader Mari Sandoz wrote, "No pleasantness here to sun-blinded eyes. Only a little valley carpeted with russet bunchgrass tucked in between towering hills whose highest dunes are bald . . . decidedly no home." The desolate landscape motivated the first homesteaders to settle as close as they could to the riverbanks where the only trees grew. Once most of the river valley land was taken, settlers had to stake claims on the treeless prairie. Without timber for constructing houses, barns, and fences, the pioneers had to make do. They cut the hard, packed earth into chunks of sod and built houses. Jokingly, they called the sod Nebraska marble. These houses, called soddies, were well suited

Mari Sandoz wrote that a neighbor's sod house "seemed to grow out of the earth and was a part of it, much as a rabbit hole in the bluff."

for the rigors of prairie life. They were cool in summer and warm in winter. Small and close to the ground, they were safer against high winds and tornadoes than wood houses. But they leaked, and if you didn't carefully seal up the cracks, mice and snakes would wriggle in.

Despite challenges, the early settlers persisted. In the rolling eastern prairies, farmers grew corn and wheat. In the western plains, ranchers raised horses, cattle, and sheep. Though people were hopeful, life was rarely easy. In 1873 and 1874, a serious drought ruined all the crops. And if that was not hardship enough, the drought was followed by a plague of grasshoppers. A newspaper columnist in Osceola, Nebraska, reported,

> The air is filled with [grasshoppers], the ground is covered with them, and the people think and talk of nothing else. It rains grasshoppers, and it snows grasshoppers. We cannot walk the streets without being struck in the face and eyes by grasshoppers, and we cannot sleep for dreaming of grasshoppers, and if the little devils don't leave for some other clime soon, we shall go grasshopper crazy.

Some people did quit the land, but many more stayed. Before the Civil War began, the population of Nebraska was only 28,841. Ten years later, it was four times as big. By 1900, the population was more than a million. Never again did Nebraska grow at such a pace.

CHANGING LIFE ON THE FARM

Near the end of the nineteenth century, the weather cooperated with farmers and rewarded their efforts. But soon other elements took their toll. Railroads charged steep shipping fees, and banks imposed high interest payments on money they loaned to farmers. Many farmers chose to fight back against unfair costs by forming new political groups. The first, called the Farmers Alliance, later became the Populist Party. Many reforms were made with the Populists' help, such as limiting banking and shipping fees. Because of the Populists' reforms and favorable weather, farmers in Nebraska in the early 1900s did very well.

The era of prosperity and hope ended in 1914 with the outbreak of World War I in Europe. In 1917, the United States joined Great Britain and its allies in their war against Germany and its allies. This was a difficult time for Nebraska's many German immigrants. In America, some people felt threatened by anything German. German words such as *sauerkraut* and *wiener* were changed to *liberty cabbage* and *hot dog*. German farmers in Nebraska were encouraged to speak only English and to become American citizens.

During the war, more than 57,000 Nebraskans served in the military. Meanwhile, back home the government encouraged farmers with the slogan "Wheat will win the war!" Prices increased and Nebraskans harvested record crops.

The war ended, and it seemed a new era of farming had arrived. Tractors and combines replaced horse-drawn farm machinery. Electricity and roads reached out to isolated farms and rural villages. But in 1929, the stock market crashed, and many people lost all their wealth. The decade that followed is called the Great Depression. Nebraska farmers did not suffer as much as others at first, because their wealth was in land rather than in stocks. But the 1930s ushered in a numbing drought. Clouds of dust swirled

In his book The Great Plains, *Ian Frazier described the first big storm of the Dust Bowl era: "Cloud darkness was total. People in the cloud's path thought the end of the world had come."*

across the plains during what is known as the Dust Bowl era. Retired music teacher Ann Peterson recalls, "The dust was so bad it was gray the whole day. Morning the same as night." Many farmers could not survive the drought. More than 65,000

Nebraskans called it quits. They packed up their belongings and set out for California, abandoning 600,000 acres of farmland.

By the time rain fell at the end of the decade, farmers had learned a few lessons. Their most valuable resource, their land, had dried up and blown away. It was time to conserve. Farmers planted trees to slow the wind and hold the earth in place, rotated their crops to keep the land healthy, and used water and irrigation methods more carefully. Slowly, the state healed.

But, in 1941, war again interrupted progress. Thousands of Nebraska farm boys enlisted in the military and went off to fight World War II. Those who didn't worked in the fields to produce food for people at home and abroad. Men and women worked in assembly lines manufacturing weapons and machinery. At the Martin Bomber plant in what is now Offutt Air Force Base, outside of Omaha, military planes were built, including the *Enola Gay* and the *Bocks Car*—the two B-29s that carried the atomic bombs dropped on Japan that ended the war.

After the war, Offutt Air Force Base, a former frontier outpost, grew in international importance. The Strategic Air Command (SAC) was created in 1946, with headquarters at Offutt. The SAC was the technical command center of the U.S. Air Force. In 1992, it was replaced with the U.S. Strategic Command, or STRATCOM, which oversees the nuclear missiles of both the air force and the navy. The United States controls its nuclear arsenal from deep under the ground at Offutt in Omaha.

Because SAC and STRATCOM have needed the most advanced technology, Omaha has become a national center for telecommunications. Technological advances have also helped improve many farming techniques. The 55,000 farms and ranches in Nebraska are some of the most successful in the world. One Nebraska farmer can feed more than 120 people each year. Together, farmers, ranchers, and city dwellers are building what many bumper stickers proclaim: "Nebraska . . . the Good Life."

At the Martin Bomber plant south of Omaha, airplanes such as this B-29 Superfortress were built.

3 EQUALITY BEFORE THE LAW

The capitol in Lincoln

"Equality before the law" is more than the Nebraska state motto. It is a way of life, a historic part of the way society works. A sense of fairness has long played a role in Nebraska government.

INSIDE GOVERNMENT

During territorial days, the Platte River divided Nebraskans politically into "North Platters" and "South Platters." When Omaha became the territorial capital, South Platters were not happy. They even threatened to secede and become citizens of Kansas. South Platters and North Platters argued until Nebraska became the thirty-seventh state in 1867. Then, the first governor chose a small village south of the Platte as the new capital city. He changed the town's name to Lincoln. The state government in Lincoln today has three branches: executive, judicial, and legislative.

Executive. The executive branch has six offices. The governor, lieutenant governor, secretary of state, state treasurer, auditor of public accounts, and the attorney general are each elected for four-year terms. The governor, who is the head of state, has many duties. He or she prepares the yearly budget and signs bills into law, or rejects them with a veto. The lieutenant governor acts as president of the legislature and assistant to the governor. If the governor is unable to serve, the lieutenant governor acts as governor.

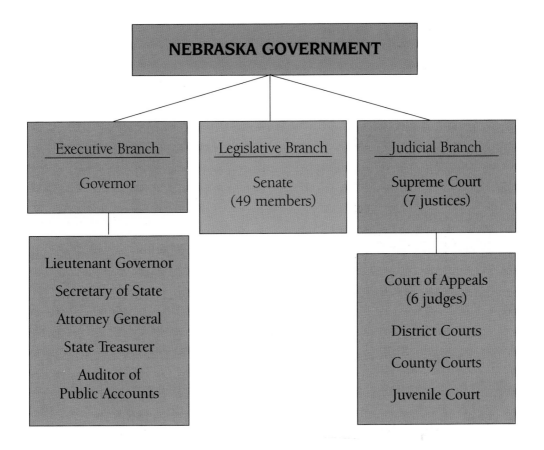

NEBRASKA GOVERNMENT

Executive Branch

Governor

Lieutenant Governor

Secretary of State

Attorney General

State Treasurer

Auditor of
Public Accounts

Legislative Branch

Senate
(49 members)

Judicial Branch

Supreme Court
(7 justices)

Court of Appeals
(6 judges)

District Courts

County Courts

Juvenile Court

Judicial. The court system is made up of a supreme court, a court of appeals, and district and county courts. Judges serve two-year terms. The supreme court has a chief justice and six associate justices. The governor appoints them from a list recommended by a legal committee. While the chief justice can be from anywhere in the state, each of the other six judges must represent one of six districts. Together, they hear cases that involve challenges to the state constitution, life imprisonment, or the death penalty. They also supervise lawyers practicing in the state and make certain that mistakes are not made in the other courts.

Twelve district courts hear the serious cases that are not heard by the supreme court. Minor cases are heard in the twelve county courts. If someone is unhappy with a district or county court ruling, he or she can request that the decision be reviewed by the court of appeals. Sometimes cases are appealed again to the supreme court.

Legislative. Nebraska citizens may have been quarrelsome at the start, but today they have a uniquely undivided state government. The federal government and every state in the nation except Nebraska has a legislature with two houses of government, usually a house of representatives and a senate. Nebraska has only one. This system is called a unicameral legislature. The forty-nine members, called senators, serve four-year terms.

In 1937, Nebraskans adopted its one-house system with no political parties. They believed the system would make government less complicated and more efficient. Nebraska statesman George Norris supported the "Nebraska experiment" in the 1930s. He argued that the states had two houses because they had copied the British system. In Britain, the king or queen appointed law-makers to the House of Lords and the people voted lawmakers to the other house of government, the House of Commons. Senator Norris argued that such a system was unnecessary in the United States, explaining, "The Constitutions of our various states are built upon the idea that there is but one class. If this be true, there is no sense or reason in having the same thing done twice, especially if it is to be done by two bodies of men elected in the same way and having the same jurisdiction."

The unicameral legislature, or "Unicam," works very well for

Nebraska. Because there are fewer members of the legislature and sessions are shorter, the Unicam saves Nebraska taxpayers money. Unicam politics supports a spirit of cooperation among senators. Since the senators do not run as Democrats, Republicans, or Independents, they have no political party to influence their activity. Senators make their own decisions and work with a variety of legislators.

Nebraska is one of a few states that allow citizens to suggest laws. In Nebraska, any person or group can bring a proposal to a senator. After information about the proposal is collected and costs are considered, the senator presents the bill to all the senators. If a majority agree that the bill has merit, then it is debated and voted on again. If the majority again votes for the bill, it is given to the governor. The bill becomes law after the governor signs it. If the governor vetoes the bill, it can still become law if thirty senators agree.

POLITICAL DIVIDE

While political parties may not divide Nebraska voters, geography does. Needs are very different for citizens in opposite ends of the state. "All the power is in Omaha," says a western Nebraska shopkeeper. For the most part, that is true. Most voters live in the east. Most of the money is also there. As a matter of fact, one of the richest men in the entire world, Warren Buffett, controls his corporate empire from an office in Omaha. Such an imbalance of wealth and population puts the western part of the state at a disadvantage.

One major issue dividing east and west is land. All land in Nebraska is taxed under similar rules. But because a western

Omaha has gracefully changed from a city of sawmills and soap factories to a leader in insurance, information management, and high-tech industries.

rancher needs to own more land to earn a living than an eastern farmer or a city dweller, the rancher pays more in taxes. The legislature is working on this complicated problem. But people in the west don't expect relief anytime soon. "Out here in the Panhandle, people talk about seceding and becoming part of

Wyoming. We have a lot more in common with Cheyenne than Omaha," laments one resident.

NEBRASKANS AT WORK

Eastern Nebraska cities are booming. The unemployment rate there is one of the lowest in the country. Homes cost less than in other urban areas, and with plentiful jobs and good schools and high-

Western Nebraska cattle ranchers face very different problems than people living in Omaha or Lincoln.

TEN LARGEST CITIES

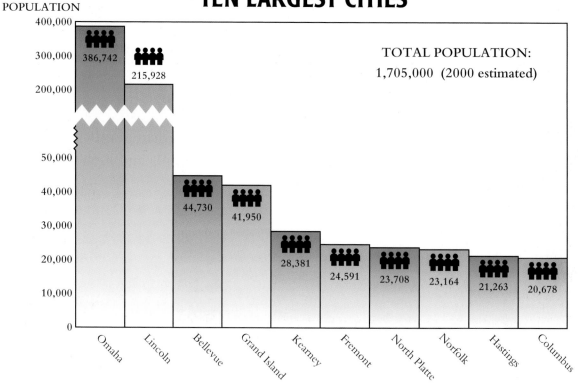

POPULATION

TOTAL POPULATION:
1,705,000 (2000 estimated)

400,000
300,000 — 386,742
215,928
200,000

50,000
40,000 — 44,730
41,950
30,000
28,381
20,000 — 24,591   23,708   23,164
21,263   20,678
10,000
0

Omaha · Lincoln · Bellevue · Grand Island · Kearney · Fremont · North Platte · Norfolk · Hastings · Columbus

ways, people are moving in. More than 40,000 have relocated to Omaha in the past decade to work at major corporations such as MCI-WorldCom, Lucent Technologies, Avaya Communications, Gallup pollsters, and Mutual of Omaha Insurance. Omaha is a leader in the country's telecommunications industry and home to many highly educated scientists. Lincoln, too, abounds in technical and professional jobs. Major employers in the state capital are the

With six thousand acres of parks and seventy-two miles of hiking and biking trails, Lincoln appeals to many newcomers.

EARNING A LIVING

Manufacturing

Grain products

Meat products

Machinery

Scientific and medical instruments

Natural Resources

Oil

Sand & gravel

Agriculture

Beef Cattle

Dairy Cattle

Corn

Grain sorghum

Hay

Hogs

Oats

Poultry

Soybeans

Sugar beets

Wheat

A FROZEN NOTION

After Thanksgiving in 1953, the C. A. Swanson & Sons Company of Omaha, Nebraska, had a lot of leftover turkey—520,000 pounds of it, to be exact. That was more than their warehouse could hold, so the meat sat in refrigerated railroad cars and crisscrossed the country. Lucky for the Swansons, they had hired Gerry Thomas, who came up with a revolutionary idea. Using metal serving trays he had seen on an airline, he and a chef prepared a turkey dinner that they quickly froze. Thomas called his idea Swanson's TV Dinners.

At first, no one thought it would amount to much. The company thought people wanted home-cooked meals. And who watched television at dinnertime? Store managers didn't think much of the TV dinner idea either, but they thought homemakers would buy them anyway, in order to use the metal trays to store buttons and other small items. Boy, were they wrong! By the end of 1954, C. A. Swanson & Sons had sold ten million Swanson's TV Dinners. In 1997, an executive with the company declared, "They're part of American culture." They certainly are. The first metal tray from Gerry Thomas's inventive solution to leftover turkey is on display in the Smithsonian Institution in Washington, D.C.

Nebraska is one of two states that grow nearly all the world's popcorn.

University of Nebraska, Novartis Ag, a pharmaceutical company, and Goodyear Tire and Rubber. With shady streets and wide boulevards, Lincoln is attracting many new residents.

Agriculture-related manufacturing is an important part of the state's economy. This includes food processing and the manufacture of fertilizers and farm machinery. Nebraska has little mining. Its main resources are petroleum and natural gas. Cement, sand, gravel, and stone also come from Nebraska.

Indeed, soil is easily Nebraska's greatest natural resource. Ranking fourth in the nation in agricultural production, Nebraska's hard-working farmers produce grain, alfalfa, cattle, corn, sorghum, and pinto beans worth billions of dollars.

But with its constant uncertainties, farming is a difficult life, and it's always changing. "Family farms are bigger now. There's less

Wheat is ready to harvest when plants turn from green to golden yellow.

manpower and more machinery," says Sidney city manager Gary Person. Farm machines are expensive but also very efficient. So when the weather is good, farmers raise huge crops and can harvest them quickly and get them to market. However, bumper crops create a surplus that lowers prices. Farmer Sandra Block of Wilcox laments, "We're not doing really well. It's like everywhere. Prices are way down." In 1999, many Nebraska farm families needed emergency aid from the federal government. When the weather is

As many as 6.7 million head of cattle are raised on Nebraska farms and ranches.

GROSS STATE PRODUCT: $53.8 BILLION

(2000 extimated)

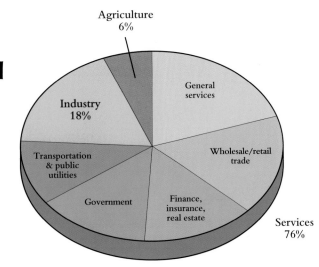

Agriculture 6%

General services

Industry 18%

Wholesale/retail trade

Transportation & public utilities

Government

Finance, insurance, real estate

Services 76%

bad, prices go up, but then farmers fear crop failure. "This has been one of the driest years ever. It reminds me of the Dust Bowl days. . . . I am really worried about our farmers around here," confides Battle Creek resident Ann Peterson.

Among the main concerns of cattle ranchers is making sure that their livetock have adequate food and water. The high plains grasses are rich in nutrients, so ranchers do not give cattle extra feed. But they need to share the rangeland fairly. "There's a lot of peer pressure around here to not overgraze the land," says Ruthann Knudsen, who lives in the Panhandle. "Cows make it or they don't." Ranchers in dry-land Nebraska do have the benefit of the enormous Ogallala Aquifer. Windmills dot the landscape, pumping water for livestock. But many people are concerned that more water has been drawn in the last decade than ever before. Knudsen supports her neighbors, however. "I think the ranchers out here are pretty good resource managers," she says. "They conserve the land and treat it with respect."

4 CITY AND COUNTRY

A telephone lineman holds up his finger and thumb to measure a distance less than an inch and describes his hometown of Mullen, Nebraska, as "this far from nowhere." Likewise, the good-natured folks of Ainsworth hold a festival every June called the Middle of Nowhere Trail Ride. Joking aside, Nebraskans know their state really is somewhere. "I could never leave," says a Lincoln librarian, "everything we need is right here."

CITY FOLKS

Although Nebraska ranks just thirty-sixth in population among the states, most Nebraskans don't live in isolation. Close to half of the population lives in two large cities, Lincoln and Omaha. Both are growing rapidly. Downtown Omaha is pushing up high-rise office complexes, renovating older portions of the city, and expanding highways. Cultural and arts organizations are thriving. Attendance is surging at the Henry Doorly Zoo, Omaha Children's Museum, Joslyn Art Museum, El Museo Latino, Great Plains Black Museum, and symphony, opera, theater, and dance companies. Visitors enjoy popular events such as River City Roundup and the Nebraska Shakespeare Festival.

Lincoln, too, is stretching its boundaries. New neighborhoods are sprouting up, providing homes for incoming families. "The suburbs

The Joslyn Art Museum has a distinguished collection of Western art and artifacts.

are growing so fast," says one retiree. "It used to be that our young people would grow up in Lincoln and hardly wait to leave. But now they get out to L.A. or Dallas and look around, and think Lincoln doesn't seem so bad after all!"

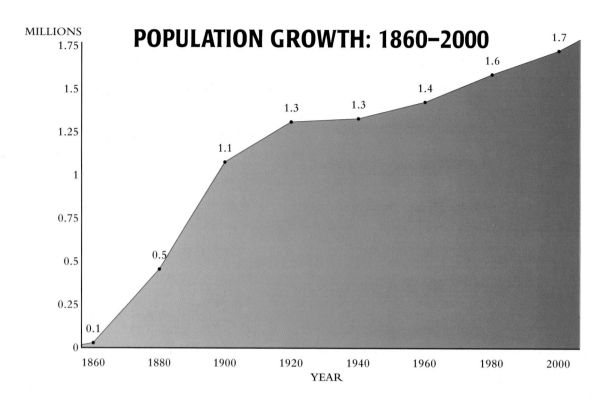

POPULATION GROWTH: 1860–2000

MILLIONS

1.7
1.6
1.4
1.3
1.3
1.1
0.5
0.1

1860 1880 1900 1920 1940 1960 1980 2000

YEAR

FRIENDLY TOWNS AND FACES

While most Nebraskans live in or near large or medium-sized cities, some prefer life in small towns or rural areas. "It's the best life there is," insists Panhandle rancher Lil Morava. "Even though in dry years it's bitter, I would never trade it for living down in Scottsbluff."

In eastern Nebraska, towns and farms are not far from each other. But in western Nebraska, you can travel on empty roads for miles before seeing a town, house, or driveway. "Look at the addresses by the driveways when you go out west," advises a Nebraska City native, "No street names; they just mark the township, range and section numbers." But whether people have next-door neighbors or live twenty miles from the nearest ranch, a sense of community prevails. People are friendly. "That's why we live here," says Heather Kreifel of Nebraska City. "We moved down from Columbus. Here, the town is small enough that everyone knows who you are, and no one is in such a hurry that they honk their horn at you if you don't take a right turn at a red light." Indeed, road manners in rural Nebraska are gracious. On long, flat stretches of open road, drivers passing one another nearly always wave, clearly saying, "Hello, fellow traveler!"

Residents of rural Nebraska communities say friendliness is a big plus to living in a small town.

But there are downsides to small-town life. While content with her western Nebraska roots, student Addy Raymer confesses, "There's pluses and minuses to living out here. The scenery is beautiful and the wildlife and recreation is more than people think it is. But even though people pull together and try to help, if there is an emergency, it's difficult to get trained medics quickly. There are a lot of agricultural accidents, and it takes a long time to airlift someone to Rapid City or Denver."

HEARTLAND HOME

Over the centuries, people from all over the world have come to Nebraska to make their home. Among the earliest were the Pawnee, Oto, Missouri, Omaha, and Ponca Indians. Later, Winnebago, Cheyenne, and others joined them. Today, approximately nine thousand Native Americans live in Nebraska. About four thousand live on the Omaha, Ponca, Winnebago, and Santee Sioux reservations.

The first large group of European settlers in Nebraska was German. Later, the railroads advertised in Europe that land was free in the American West, so Czech, Swedish, Danish, Russian, and Irish immigrants followed. The promise of opportunity lured people from other regions. African-American families moved to the state after the Civil War. When farms and ranches needed more workers, many Latinos migrated. In recent years, people from

Nebraskans of Latin American ancestry are surpassing African Americans as Nebraska's largest minority group.

Vietnam, Cambodia, the Middle East, and Central America have left their strife-ridden nations for a new chance in America. Many have immigrated to Lincoln. "We have very active religious communities who work hard to sponsor refugees," says Lincoln resident Josie Sheffield. Citizens donate everything the newcomers need to get started. Several organizations help find jobs, schools, and permanent homes. As newsman Brad Penner reported, "They'll find a helping hand in Nebraska."

HEYDAYS AND HOLIDAYS

"The spirit of a people lives in its history" is engraved on the wall of the Nebraska State Historical Society. Nebraskans love to celebrate their heritage. One favorite holiday is Arbor Day, which was born in Nebraska City. People flock into town to enjoy barbecues, music, and environmental exhibits, and of course, to plant trees. "I packaged up 800 seedlings myself this year," muses one Nebraska City businesswoman. "We're expecting a lot of kids; this is our biggest event."

Just about every little town boasts some unique celebration. The Blue Sky Jubilee in the small farming community of Anselmo has turtle and bicycle races, square dances, and even a greased pig contest. Sheep farmer Kim Lucas says, "They grease a pig and set it loose with the kids. But most of the kids wind up falling on each other and the pig goes scot free!"

Festivals commemorating Nebraska's past include Oregon Trail Days in Scottsbluff and Gering, Fur Trade Days in Chadron, and Wild West rodeos near Buffalo Bill's ranch in North Platte. At

THE TREE PLANTER'S STATE

Before becoming famous as the Cornhusker State, Nebraska was nicknamed the Tree Planter's State, and for very good reason. In the 1850s, a man named J. Sterling Morton became the editor of the Nebraska City newspaper. He was passionate about growing crops and planting trees. Morton encouraged farmers and ranchers to plant mostly native trees such as cottonwood, maple, box elder, and ash. He advised them to dig up saplings growing along the riverbanks and replant them on their farms. In 1885, the newspaper held a competition and offered a reward. That year, over a million trees were planted. The state proclaimed Morton's birthday, April 22, Arbor Day. Today, Arbor Day is sometimes combined with the holiday called Earth Day.

Morton continued inspiring farmers to plant trees. In 1869, he was the state director of agriculture. He offered a big tax break to farmers who would plant an acre of forest on their land. It was so popular that eight years later, the state treasury went broke! Although the tax break had to be canceled, many forests remain today as a result.

Tree planting didn't just happen on private land. In 1902, President Theodore Roosevelt established the Nebraska National Forest. In the desertlike Sandhills, citizens hand-planted 13 million seedlings. It is the only planted forest in the national forest system and today provides seedlings to other national forest lands that have been burned or logged.

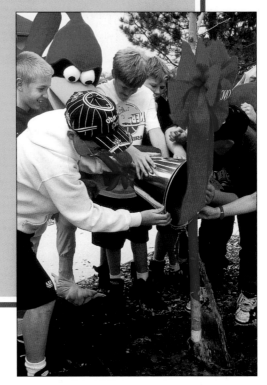

One of America's first rodeos was held by Buffalo Bill at his Scouts Rest Ranch in North Platte to celebrate the Fourth of July in 1882.

county fairs, people enjoy watching antique tractor pulls and demonstrations of pioneer life.

Ethnic celebrations are also popular. Drive into the farming town of Lexington, and the billboards announce, "Lexington—an All America City." You also see that shop signs are in English and Spanish. When a large meat-processing plant was built in 1990, many Latinos moved to Lexington to work. Now the growing city is nearly one-quarter Latino. Each May, Lexington celebrates its heritage with Latin dancing and Mexican music at a Cinco de Mayo festival.

There are many other ethnic celebrations you wouldn't want to miss. For more than fifty years, Verdigre has sponsored its mouth-watering Kolache Days event, starring the delicious Czech fruit-filled pastries called kolache. You can get a second helping in August, when Wilber, which calls itself the Czech Capital of Nebraska, hosts the Nebraska Czech Festival. Other fun-filled ethnic festivals are the Greek Festival in Bridgeport, St. Patrick's Day in O'Neill, and the Danish celebration Grundlovsfest in Dannebrog.

The oldest ongoing celebration in Nebraska is a powwow on the

ETHNIC NEBRASKA

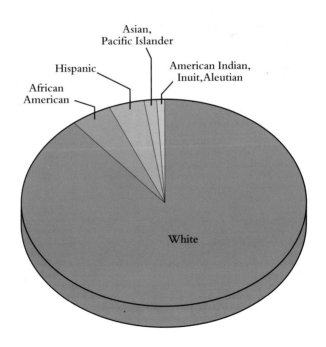

Asian, Pacific Islander

Hispanic

American Indian, Inuit, Aleutian

African American

White

KOLACHE

The Czechs and Slovaks of Nebraska celebrate their heritage with accordion music and kolache. While you may not be prepared to start kicking up your heels, you should never turn down a kolache!

    1 cup milk
    1 packet yeast
    3 tablespoons sugar
    1 teaspoon salt
    1 egg, beaten
    ¼ cup shortening
    3 cups flour
    fruit preserve

Warm one cup milk and pour it into a bowl. Dissolve yeast, sugar, and salt in the milk. Add the beaten egg and shortening. Mix well. Add flour and stir thoroughly.

Let the mixture rise. Form it into 2-inch balls. Place them on a greased pan and brush with melted shortening. Let rise until doubled in size. Make depressions with your thumb for the filling. Fill with preserve and let rise until puffy. Bake at 400 degrees for 12 minutes.

Mmmmmmm, you may want to dance to accordion music after all!

Recent immigrants have brought traditional Latin American celebrations to Nebraska.

Wilber's Nebraska Czech Festival has grown every year since it began in 1962.

Omaha reservation called Umonhon Harvest Hethushka. Powwows
celebrate Native American culture with dance, music, chants, food,
and traditional crafts. During the main event, everyone gathers
around a large circle to watch dancers perform. The dancers wear

costumes decorated with beads and feathers, which have passed from generation to generation. The music is also handed down. One year, Omaha songs recorded more than a century ago were played for the crowd. Many Omahas said, "I know that song, we still sing that song!" Another important part of the powwow is the

Wearing traditional costumes and accompanied by drums and chants, Lakota dancers pass on legends and cultural traditions through song and dance.

"giveaway." During this ceremony, the hosts honor their guests by offering gifts, usually blankets or food baskets. Native Americans have a strong sense of generosity, and often a giveaway lasts quite awhile!

THE SPORTING LIFE

It is hard to be in Nebraska and not know when it is "game day," that is, the day the University of Nebraska Cornhuskers play

On game day, the fans filling Memorial Stadium wear the University of Nebraska school colors and turn Lincoln into a sea of red.

football. On game day, spectators, outfitted in the school colors of red and white, engulf Lincoln. Across Nebraska and beyond, Cornhusker fans are enthusiastic. Whether seated in the stadium or watching the game on television, Nebraskans all join together on game day to cheer, "Go, Big Red!"

Ask a Nebraskan, "What do you like to do here?" and you get a variety of responses, but most of them will have something to do with the out-of-doors. Nebraskans love to fish, hunt, cycle, and sail. Yes, in the land once called the Great American Desert, boating is a favorite sport. A surprising number of driveways yield up a boat and trailer ready to ply the waters of giant Lake McConaughy, or any of the hundreds of other lakes and reservoirs in the state. Canoeists and kayakers cannot say enough good about the 11,000 miles of Nebraska rivers and streams. Troy Nutter of the Sandhills says with a smile, "I love the Dismal River, it's so remote, you can get in a canoe and go five or six hours and never see anybody else." Innkeeper Jeanne Goetzinger agrees that the Nebraska wilderness is special. Mountain bikers and hunters come from all over America to stay in her small hotel in Chadron near the Pine Ridge. She says, "When I get in the hills, I know I am alive—it's a privilege to be here."

5 SEEKERS AND CHAMPIONS

An Omaha creation myth says that before humans were earth-bound, they were spirits that moved about in space between the earth and the stars. Once they found a home on the plains, the land vibrated with their expressions of joy. Many native Nebraskans reflect their "heavenly" origins—some became stars.

HE AIN'T HEAVY

In 1904, a young man left Ireland, bound for America. He hoped to become a Catholic priest. By 1912, Father Edward J. Flanagan was pastor of St. Patrick's Church in downtown Omaha.

In those times, life was bitter hard. Farms failed, and many men left the land to look for work. But they seldom fared any better in the city, and often became hungry and homeless. Father Flanagan eased their suffering by making room for forty men in a vacant hotel. Within six weeks, half of the men had jobs. By 1917, the hotel contained three hundred beds and an employment agency. Still, Father Flanagan was discouraged. He saw men lose their jobs and drift back into homelessness. Father Flanagan wrote,

> In talking with the men I learned that they were orphaned in childhood . . . or they were members of large families where income was not sufficient to care for them. They veered here, they were shoved there, . . . and were now shells of men. . . . I knew

The story of Father Flanagan inspired the Academy Award–winning movie, Boys Town.

that my work was not with these shells of men, but with . . . the homeless waifs who had nowhere to turn, no one to guide them.

In other words, Father Flanagan decided to prevent homeless boys from becoming homeless men. In December 1917, he borrowed ninety dollars and rented a house. Boys arrived daily, and in two weeks, there were twenty-five. In a few months, he was caring for over a hundred boys. He turned no one away. Their space soon became cramped, so Father Flanagan bought a 160-acre farm outside Omaha.

Father Flanagan and the boys built houses, barns, a school, and small factories on the land that became known as Boys Town. Boys were expected to attend school, help with chores, and learn a trade. But it was not all work. Father Flanagan felt that play, too, was each boy's right. He made certain the boys learned sports and sportsmanship.

Teamwork and feeling like part of a family were important for the boys. In the middle of the grounds today stands a sculpture called *Two Brothers*. It was based on a photograph of two Boys Town residents on a field trip. On the day the photo was taken, an older boy noticed that a younger one wearing leg braces was being left behind. The older one lifted the younger one onto his back and carried him. The base of the sculpture reads, "He ain't heavy, Father . . . he's m' brother."

Boys Town, now called Girls and Boys Town, continues to expand. It became its own city with a police force, a fire department, and a post office in 1936. Today, 550 boys and girls live on its 1,300 acres, and many more live in facilities in thirteen other states. Over the years, thousands of boys and girls have been loved and cared for because of Father Flanagan's dedication and faith.

WARRIOR SISTERS

In 1854, the Omaha tribe gave up 6 million acres of land and agreed to move to a small reservation on the Missouri River. Chief Iron Eye signed that treaty, believing the only way to get along with the

Besides practicing medicine, Dr. Susan La Flesche Picotte was a church and community leader who encouraged respect between races.

Americans was to adopt their ways. "Look ahead," he said, "and you will see nothing but the white man." Heeding his words, two of the chief's daughters entered the white world while seeking to improve the plight of their people.

The youngest, Susan La Flesche Picotte, became the first Native

American woman to graduate from medical school. Before attending the Woman's Medical College in Philadelphia, where she was the only Native American in her class, she studied with Omaha medicine men and women and learned about ancient healing methods that used herbs, sweat baths, songs, and prayer.

Susan returned to the Omaha reservation as a formally trained medical doctor. She traveled hundreds of miles on horseback, in summer's sticky heat and winter's icy cold, caring for Native Americans and whites alike. She never turned anyone down, even after she developed a bone disease that made her trips painful. She declared, "I owe my people a responsibility."

Picotte served her people in other ways as well. After the federal government took over the Omaha's tribal finances, Picotte wrote many letters. In 1910, she went to Washington, D.C., and convinced government officials that the Omahas were capable of managing their own money and property. She so impressed everyone that the *New York Sun* newspaper proclaimed her the "virtual Chief" of the Omaha.

Picotte knew that she did not have long to live. As illness tapped her strength, she worked all the harder to raise funds to build a community hospital. At last, in 1913, Picotte's dream was realized. Sadly, she lived only two more years. It is said that in her twenty-five years as a physician she had treated every single member of her tribe. To this day, the Dr. Susan La Flesche Picotte Center is a symbol of a remarkable woman's love for her people.

Susan's older sister, Susette La Flesche, was born the year their father signed the treaty creating their reservation. Following Iron Eye's belief that the future lay in the white man's ways, Susette attended a boarding school run by whites, where speaking her native language was forbidden. She then enrolled in the Elizabeth Institute for Young Ladies in New Jersey. There, her keen writing ability quickly became apparent, and she was published by the *New York Tribune* while still in high school.

Like her sister, La Flesche returned home, where she began teaching. But the meager possessions of the reservation schoolhouse were a far cry from the elegant furnishings and beautifully bound books she had enjoyed in New Jersey. She threw herself into

Susette La Flesche Tibbles, or Bright Eyes, began her career as an advocate for Native Americans by interpreting for Chief Standing Bear during his landmark trial.

her work, hoping to raise the quality of life for her people through education.

La Flesche's life took a sudden turn when Chief Standing Bear of the Ponca tribe asked the Omaha for help. The U.S. government had ordered the Ponca to Indian Territory in Oklahoma. Standing Bear wanted to remain in Nebraska. La Flesche resented the government's attitude that Indian people were inferior and could be pushed around at will. She wrote letters to sympathetic whites that were so persuasive she was invited to speak to gatherings in New York and Massachusetts. There she was known by her Indian name, Bright Eyes, and was befriended by several important figures, among them writers Louisa May Alcott, Mark Twain, and Henry Wadsworth Longfellow. In her speeches, she requested equal rights and U.S. citizenship for Native Americans, declaring,

> Your government has no right to say to us, "Go here, or Go there," and if we show any reluctance, to force us to do its will at the point of the bayonet. An Indian does not want to cultivate a piece of land, fence it in, build him a house, furnish and stock his farm, and just as he is ready to enjoy the fruits of it, to have it taken from him and be sent with his family to a southern clime to die. Do you wonder that the Indian feels outraged by such treatment?

Her appeals eventually helped win the Ponca's return. Bright Eyes continued to tour New England and Europe, where her words brought her acclaim. One evening, after hearing her speak, Longfellow admitted, "I've been a student of the English language all my life, and I would give all I possess if I could speak with the simplicity, fluency, and force used by that Indian girl."

LEADING THE WAY

Slavery may have ended with the Civil War, but racial discrimination remained rampant, especially in the South. Hoping for better jobs and education, many African Americans from the South moved to northern cities. Reverend Earl Little was one of them. He moved his young family to Omaha. There his son Malcolm was born. Malcolm would grow up to be one of the country's foremost African-American leaders.

The cities in the North seldom lived up to their promise. Blacks were forced to live in the poorest parts of town, were hired only for the lowest-paying jobs, and were frequently harassed by whites. Reverend Little's sermons encouraged blacks to take pride in their heritage and in the accomplishments of Africans and African nations. These sermons angered a group of intolerant whites who repeatedly attacked the family's home. By the time Malcolm was six, his father was dead.

Malcolm's family fell apart after this, and Malcolm eventually went to live with a relative in the East. At age seventeen, he was sent to jail for burglary. While in jail, he learned about a religion called the Nation of Islam. When Malcolm left jail, he turned away from crime and joined the Nation of Islam.

Islam is a religion practiced by millions in Africa, the Middle East, and Asia. Followers of the Nation of Islam uphold many of Islam's ways. But to those ways, they add a belief that white people stole everything from black people—their freedom, knowledge of their past, even their true names. In America, the last names of most blacks had originally belonged to a slave master. Ethnic

Malcolm X delivered hundreds of memorable speeches. In 1965 he declared, "You can't separate peace from freedom because no one can be at peace unless he has his freedom."

names from Africa were forgotten. Members of the Nation of Islam resented having a "slave name," so they replaced their surnames with a simple "X." Thus, Malcolm Little became Malcolm X.

Malcolm inherited his father's talent for public speaking. His passion and faith inspired thousands of Americans to take pride in their African heritage. Because he brought so many new members to the fold, he was appointed minister of the Harlem temple in New York City, the Nation of Islam's largest congregation. It was there that Malcolm X became a national figure.

As Malcolm's power and influence grew, Elijah Mohammed, the leader of the Nation of Islam, began to feel threatened by him. The two men had a bitter falling out. In 1964, Malcolm X resigned. Looking for guidance, he took a pilgrimage to Mecca, Saudi Arabia, the Islamic holy city. There, he met a white Islamic holy man who preached brotherhood and love. Again transformed, Malcolm took another new name, this time a traditional Islamic name, El-Hajj Malik El-Shabazz. This name is the one his family carries today.

When Malcolm X returned to America, he became an ardent spokesperson for the rights of black citizens. But on February 21, 1965, Malcolm X was assassinated. Reflecting on his life, Alex Haley, who cowrote *The Autobiography of Malcolm X*, said he was "valiant beyond belief."

SONGS OF THE LARK

Even by today's standards, the area in Nebraska called the Divide is a faraway place. This lonely expanse of plains between the Republican and the Little Blue Rivers is not easy to get to even with modern means of transportation. Yet in 1883, Willa Cather's family wended their way from Virginia to the Divide and built a home.

In addition to novels, stories, newspaper articles and essays, Willa Cather also wrote poetry. One Cather poem begins: "Red the pasture ridges gleamed/Where the sun was sinking/Slow the windmill rasped and wheezed/Where the herd was drinking."

Young Willa was completely unprepared for this new country. Though Nebraska was a state by then, the plains and prairies were nonetheless remote and wild. Willa would later pen, "There seemed to be nothing to see; no fences, no creeks or trees, no hills or fields. If there was a road, I could not make it out in the faint starlight. There was nothing but land, not a country at all, but the material out of which countries are made." She was homesick for the forests of Virginia. When her mother became ill, Willa grew

TIME FRAMED

Solomon Devoe Butcher was not cut out for homesteading. He tried it by moving to Custer County with his father and brother in 1880. But Solomon was too restless to farm the plains. So he and his young wife moved to the little town of Walworth, and he began to teach school. After saving as much money as he could, he bought a camera and rigged up a wagon. Then he took to the road—actually, to the muddy ruts of rural Custer County. All around him, people were homesteading, building crude houses out of sod and trying to coax a living from the land. Solomon was there, asking questions and taking pictures. He left over 3,500 pictures as his legacy, telling the tale of homesteading the Great Plains like no other. Solomon never felt that his life was successful, but what he captured on film and in his field notes makes him unforgettable.

more lonesome in their adopted home. Trying to ease her sadness, Willa's father gave her a pony. The creature opened her world. She rode the immense distances between neighboring farms and visited the women homesteaders. These brave and solitary European immigrants, with their unfamiliar languages and remarkable courage, later sprang to life as characters in Cather's many stories and novels. In such acclaimed books as *O Pioneers!*, *My Antonia*, and *Song of the Lark*, she showed herself to be one of the finest spokespersons for life on the plains.

AN ALL-AMERICAN HERO

Ask any Nebraska football fan (and in Nebraska, that is just about anybody) who they would call a modern-day hero. "Coach Tom Osborne," will be the reply. Tom Osborne is a born and bred Nebraskan. He was raised in the small western Nebraska town of Hastings. When he graduated from Hastings College in 1959, his skill on the football field earned him the statewide title Athlete of the Year. Soon after, he was drafted into the National Football League and played three seasons as a wide receiver.

In 1962, Osborne and his wife returned home. While a graduate student at the University of Nebraska in Lincoln, Osborne started coaching football part-time. By 1973, he was the University of Nebraska Cornhuskers head coach. He soon became adored by football fans across the state. In his thirty-six years as coach, his teams won thirteen conference crowns and five national titles. During the last five years that Tom Osborne coached the Cornhuskers, they won sixty out of sixty-three games. Because of his amazing accom-

Former Cornhusker coach Tom Osborne began his political career as a freshman member of the 107th U.S. Congress in 2001.

plishments, the College Football Hall of Fame inducted Osborne right away, without waiting the usual three years after a coach's retirement.

But Osborne did not retire for long. In the year 2000, he entered the race for one of Nebraska's three U.S. congressional seats. "Tom Osborne is a guy with a lot of integrity and real common sense," says one western Nebraska voter. "People know they can trust him." In his first political election ever, Osborne received an astounding 75 percent of the vote. A Chadron restaurant owner declared, "Everybody loves him. The people running against him should just give up."

6 THE OPEN ROAD

I-80 is one of the country's busiest east-west highways, slicing border to border across Nebraska. But traveling on it won't really take you far, as Omaha native Jim Royer is quick to tell you: "You gotta get off the interstate if you want to see anything." That turns out to be good advice to follow.

RIVER JOURNEYS

The earliest and easiest way to travel Nebraska was by water. Follow the river roads today and you will see some of Nebraska's most historic sights. The mighty Missouri wends along the eastern part of the state. An interesting river town is Nebraska City. There you will find the stately Arbor Lodge, home of Arbor Day's founder, J. Sterling Morton. It is also the site of Abraham Kagi's simple pioneer cabin. In 1851, Kagi built a small log cabin near Table Creek. Underneath, he dug a root cellar. Connected to the cellar was a tunnel that led to the creek. Abraham Kagi was actually an anti-slavery activist. His "root cellar" was a link in the Underground Railroad and provided a safe haven for fugitive slaves traveling north to freedom. Today, the tiny home is still furnished as it was in Kagi's time, and you can see this important piece of history when you visit the site now called John Brown's Cave.

No river is more identified with Nebraska than the Platte. This

PLACES TO SEE

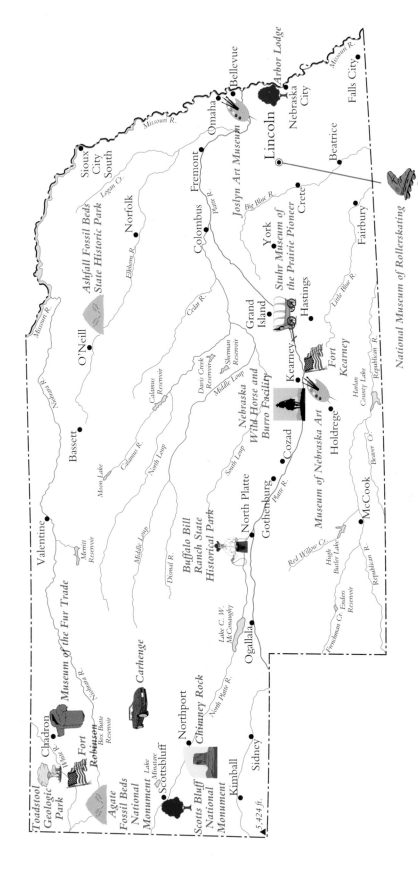

Toadstool Geologic Park
Museum of the Fur Trade
Chadron
Fort Robinson
White R.
Box Butte Reservoir
Niobrara R.
Carhenge
Agate Fossil Beds National Monument
Minatare Lake
Scottsbluff
Northport
Chimney Rock
Scotts Bluff National Monument
Kimball
Sidney
5,424 ft.

Valentine
Merritt Reservoir
Dismal R.
Middle Loup
Lake C. W. McConaughy
Ogallala
North Platte R.
North Platte
Gothenburg
Buffalo Bill Ranch State Historical Park
Cozad
Platte R.
Red Willow Cr.
McCook
Hugh Butler Lake
Republican R.
Frenchman Cr. Enders Reservoir

O'Neill
Bassett
Moon Lake
Calamus R.
North Loup
Calamus Reservoir
South Loup
Davis Creek Reservoir
Sherman Reservoir
Middle Loup
Cedar R.
Nebraska Wild Horse and Burro Facility
Kearney
Fort Kearney
Holdrege
Museum of Nebraska Art
Harlan County Lake
Beaver Cr.
Republican R.

Ashfall Fossil Beds State Historic Park
Norfolk
Elkhorn R.
Logan Cr.
Columbus
Fremont
Platte R.
Grand Island
Stuhr Museum of the Prairie Pioneer
Hastings
Little Blue R.

Sioux City South
Missouri R.
Omaha
Bellevue
Arbor Lodge
Missouri R.
Nebraska City
Falls City
Joslyn Art Museum
Lincoln
York
Big Blue R.
Crete
Beatrice
Fairbury
Little Blue R.

National Museum of Rollerskating

Museum of Nebraska History

The Nebraska highway speed limit is seventy-five miles per hour, a far cry from the pace of pioneers in covered wagons who crossed the state at fifteen miles per day.

waterway flows past some of the state's foremost attractions. The Great Platte River Road carried many a pioneer west to Oregon, California, and Utah. Reminders of their journey are plentiful today. The Stuhr Museum of the Prairie Pioneer near Grand Island covers the history of Native Americans and Old West adventurers. Original structures such as a general store, a railroad depot, wooden sidewalks, and a Pawnee earth lodge have been preserved with great care. The museum feels so authentic that several movies have been filmed there, including *Sarah, Plain & Tall*, the story of a frontier girl.

Farther along the Platte River Road is Fort Kearny, which was built in 1848 to protect settlers traveling the Oregon Trail. While reliving early American military history at the fort, remember to look overhead for migrating sandhill cranes if you're visiting in the spring. If you miss the migration, try another wonderful wildlife experience at Elm Creek Wild Horse and Burro Facility. Here, wild horses and burros that have been rounded up from government-owned land are given a home.

As you continue west the land changes. You leave rolling prairie and farmland and head into the high plains. Past the town of North Platte a dam holds back the North Platte River, forming Lake McConaughy, the state's largest lake. The setting feels very remote, but the lake is teeming with boaters, campers, and out-doors enthusiasts.

Lake McConaughy has 105 miles of white sand beaches that are popular with vacationers.

In the days that mastodons roamed the area, nearby Ash Hollow was a treasured watering hole. Ancestors of the Apache lived in this sheltered valley, drank the sweet water, and enjoyed the shade of the ash trees growing in rare abundance. Pioneers passed through later, eventually fouling the water and felling the trees. Today the site has been restored. In the whispering quiet of the ash groves, there is an interpretive center and an old schoolhouse. Atop Ash Hollow, you get a breathtaking view of the surrounding ridges. From this vista, the pioneers confronted Windlass Hill, the steep west slope. While their wagons rattled wildly down the hill, pioneers had their first taste of the rugged Rocky Mountain roads waiting for them.

There are so many historic sights to see and experience along the Platte River Road, it would be easy to overlook some of them. But one sight hard to miss is Chimney Rock, outside of Scottsbluff. When pioneers plodded west, they could see this towering rock formation ahead of them for several days. Although travel is faster today, Chimney Rock remains a conspicuous landmark. Travelers have always stopped to gawk at it and other nearby formations. "I taught fourth grade for twenty-five years," says a retired Kearney schoolteacher, "and I can say Chimney Rock, Courthouse, and Jail Rocks were the best field trips we took. Kids couldn't wait to go."

Many rivers besides the Missouri and the Platte crisscross Nebraska. Follow the Dismal or the Loup through the Sandhills and you will be surrounded by wilderness. The sand dunes are dotted with rivers, streams, and lakes. Sandhills resident Troy Nutter jokes, "You get eastern Nebraskans out here and they think they are in the mountains." Nutter is not alone in his fondness for

THE SKIES OVERHEAD

"There's no darker dark than in the Sandhills," says resident Troy Nutter. When astronomers want to watch the night sky, the Sandhills are one of the first places they head. Hundreds of amateur astronomers from as far away as Puerto Rico and China enjoy the Nebraska Star Party each year near Valentine, in the heart of the Sandhills. Star parties are outdoor observing sessions that are held at remote locations to avoid the lights of urban areas. Even small towns generate what is called skyglow. The remote Sandhills give prairie astronomers the opportunity to see an array of stars and galaxies that wouldn't be visible in more populated areas.

Away from light pollution, Nebraska Star Party-goers get a fantastic view of the Milky Way galaxy, the northern lights, and meteor showers. Another exciting sight for amateur astronomers is the Cat's Eye nebula, which scientists believe to be an unusual cluster of two dying stars surrounded by a halo of gases. For star party-goers, sights such as this truly make the Nebraska night sky a marvel.

Nebraska's wilderness. Each year, tens of thousands of people visit the wild and scenic Niobrara River to canoe, hike, fish, and swim. The Niobrara rushes through six different ecosystems from grasslands to sandstone canyons, has more than ninety waterfalls, and provides a habitat for herds of deer, elk, and bison.

ANCIENT WONDERS

"I must have slept through history class," says Korinda Licking of Thedford, "because when I went up north to the Ashfall beds I

Nebraska was the first state to choose an official fossil: the mammoth. Scientists say a mammoth unearthed near Lincoln weighed fifteen tons when it was alive!

couldn't believe it!" The Ashfall Fossil Beds State Historic Park is a world-renowned archaeological site. The Niobrara River valley was once home to an incredibly diverse array of creatures that congregated around the watering holes. More than ten million years ago, a volcano erupted, spewing a cloud of ash across the land. When the ash fell over this particular watering hole, it suffocated all the animals at once and buried them. Even in a land noted for fossils, the Ashfall Fossil Beds are remarkable. Not only is it rare to find whole herds buried together, as they are here, but it is also rare that so many different creatures died at once. Prehistoric horses, camels, giant tortoises, and rhinos have all been found at the site. Many of the skeletons were discovered right next to an imprint of the animal's final footstep or with a last meal of grass in their mouths. Most of the fossils at the site are still buried. While you watch, scientists are still carefully uncovering the bones. They believe that large meat-eaters were hunting in the area, so they hope to uncover a sabertooth tiger or a beardog someday. Just think, they might brush the ash off of such a discovery on the day that you stop by!

If you follow the Niobrara River valley west, you will enter the Oglala National Grasslands. Ancient rivers, long since dried up, helped erode a portion of this landscape into winding mazes and odd, umbrella-shaped rock formations, now aptly called Toadstool Geologic Park. Fossils thirty million years old have been found in the park, including ancestors of modern dogs, cats, horses, and wild pigs. The area's fossils are of such high quality and so abundant that museums around the world exhibit them.

Head into Nebraska's western Panhandle and you will find yourself in some of the wildest and most remote country the nation has to offer. On distant hills, you may see cattle ranging and windmills pumping, but you may easily go without seeing a car, tractor, house, or driveway along the lonely stretch of road from Fort Robinson to the Agate Fossil Beds National Monument. "It's very serene," says Ruthann Knudsen, superintendent of the monument, "and there is nowhere to get to from here—we are a long way from places." But driving to Agate Fossil Beds is well worth the trip. In the 1800s, the area became popular with East Coast scientists looking for fossils. One interesting creature uncovered was Palaeocastor, a beaverlike animal that dug burrows in a corkscrew pattern. You can hike out on the Devil's Corkscrew trail and see the squirrelly prehistoric tunnels firsthand. Remains of prehistoric camels and Moropus, an

Sandstone and clay formations flank 30-million year old fossil tracks at Toadstool Geologic Park.

animal related to both the rhinoceros and the horse, were also discovered on the site.

But the history surrounding Agate Fossil Beds is more than ancient. The monument was once Agate Springs Ranch, which was owned by a frontier couple, James and Kate Cook. The Cooks and Red Cloud, a Lakota chief, became friends. At the time, there was much strife between Red Cloud's tribe and the U.S. military, and James Cook often intervened on behalf of the Lakota. To show his gratitude and to ensure that some part of the Lakota way of life was preserved, Red Cloud presented many gifts to the Cooks. Among them were ceremonial costumes, saddles, war clubs, moccasins, pipes, bows, and painted bison hides. The collection, which is on display at the park, is an astonishing representation of plains Indian life.

THE WILD WEST

"The Nebraska Panhandle's motto should be:'We're not Omaha,'" laughs Ruthann Knudsen, "because it's the West out here!" She is right. The Nebraska Panhandle is a land of cattle drives, bison herds, historic battlefields, and magnificent Great Plains scenery. Touring this region will give you frequent reasons to admire the rich history and incredible beauty of the American West.

Among the Panhandle's most spectacular sites is Fort Robinson. This fort was built in the nineteenth century to protect settlers from Indians. The great chief Crazy Horse was killed by a soldier here and chiefs Dull Knife and Red Cloud were held prisoner on the grounds. The fort was a military outpost into the twentieth

Today, most bison herds range on private land.

century, housing German prisoners during World War II. Today, the fort's bloody past stands in stark contrast to its extraordinary beauty. "Fort Rob is awesome!" claims Alliance resident Addy Raymer. "It's past isn't great, but there is just so much to do there that you just try to put your feelings aside." Fort Rob, as it is affectionately called, is located in the Pine Ridge region. Herds of bison range through canyons surrounded by high white cliffs, rugged buttes, and hills covered in deep green pines. It is located in Nebraska's most popular state park, where there is plenty to do, from horseback riding and hunting to fishing, cross-country skiing, mountain biking, and hiking.

For history of a different kind, check out the Museum of the Fur Trade in tiny Chadron. It has a phenomenal collection of weapons, beadwork, furs, costumes, and everyday supplies used by trappers and traders from 1600 to 1900. "You have to go," insists Chadron resident Jeanne Goetzinger. "There's nothing like it anywhere in the world."

There is also nothing in the world quite like visiting Dobby Lee's Frontier Town in Alliance. Lee has so many stories to tell that he is the story himself! A slightly stooped, red-cheeked, blue-eyed man in overalls, Lee has turned his home into a museum. Before he retired, he drove a school bus to athletic competitions all over the Great Plains. "I drove everywhere," he says. "We would go places and see stuff and then the next time we went, it'd be gone. That's history going down the drain. That's why I started collecting." Walking around Lee's backyard takes hours, and not because of its size. It's crowded with original frontier buildings such as a general store, a courthouse, a jail, a barber shop, the area's first gas station, and the one-room cabin of the first African Americans to homestead in the county. "You should read about Robert Ball-Anderson," says Lee. "He wrote a book called *From Slavery to Affluence* about how he went from being a Civil War veteran and former slave to a homesteader who made it rich in diamonds and real estate. Look, here's a picture of me with his wife, one of the last Civil War widows. She just died a few years back." When

You'll want to have film in your camera when you visit Carhenge.

you sit in the Andersons' cabin, now in Lee's yard, you sit on old handmade chairs. Amazingly, everything at Frontier Town is out in the open. You can touch, inspect, and explore to your heart's content.

Although Alliance is a small town, it boasts more than one unusual and inviting attraction. Just a couple of miles outside of town, in the heart of wide, flat wheat fields, is a stop-you-in-your-tracks sight. You can say that it, too, is "like no place else in the world," except that it is actually a lot like someplace else in the world, a very famous place. In England, the giant four-thousand-year-old stone circle called Stonehenge has long inspired the curious. One such person was Jim Reinders, an Alliance native, who spent several years in England. One year when he returned to Alliance, he looked at the old cars parked around the family farm. He and his relatives cooked up a scheme to recreate Stonehenge using Cadillacs and Oldsmobiles instead of rock. It turned into a huge project. They painted all the cars gray and, using cranes and forklifts, stuck them upright in the earth in the same formation as the stones in England. Carhenge rises as dramatically out of Alliance wheat fields as Stonehenge does from England's Salisbury Plain. City officials were originally displeased with what they considered an eyesore. But as word got out, tourists came from all over the world to admire Jim Reinders' amusing and monumental tribute. Once city officials realized they had a gem of an attraction on their hands, they sensibly allowed Reinders' vision to stand.

Carhenge is a fine representation of Nebraska and its people—original, hardworking, agreeable, and quietly, very worldly-wise. It is another good reason to get to know Nebraska.

THE FLAG: The state flag was designed in 1925 and officially adopted in 1963. It shows the Nebraska seal in gold and silver in the center of a blue background.

THE SEAL: The Nebraska seal shows symbols of the state's history and economy: a worker with a hammer and anvil, a cabin and sheaves of grain, a steamboat traveling up the Missouri River, and a train heading toward the Rocky Mountains. On a banner above these scenes is the state motto, Equality Before the Law. Surrounding the entire seal are the words the Great Seal of the State of Nebraska and the date March 1, 1867, when Nebraska entered the Union and the seal was adopted.

STATE SURVEY

Statehood: March 1, 1867

Origin of Name: From the Oto Indian word *nebrathka*, which means "flat water." It was the tribe's name for Nebraska's main river, the Platte.

Nickname: Cornhusker State

Capital: Lincoln

Motto: Equality before the Law

Bird: Western meadowlark

Mammal: White-tailed deer

Fish: Channel catfish

Flower: Goldenrod

Western meadowlark

White-tailed deer

Goldenrod

BEAUTIFUL NEBRASKA

"Beautiful Nebraska" was adopted as the official state song in 1967.

Grass: Little bluestem

Tree: Cottonwood

Insect: Honeybee

Stone: Prairie agate

Gemstone: Blue chalcedoney

Fossil: Mammoth

GEOGRAPHY

Highest Point: 5,426 feet above sea level, in Kimball County

Lowest Point: 840 feet above sea level, in Richardson County

Area: 77,359 square miles

Greatest Distance, North to South: 206 miles

Greatest Distance, East to West: 462 miles

Bordering States: South Dakota to the north, Colorado and Wyoming to the west, Kansas to the south, Iowa and Missouri to the east

Hottest Recorded Temperature: 118°F at Minden on July 24, 1936, at Hartington on July 17, 1936, and at Geneva on July 15, 1934

Coldest Recorded Temperature: -47°F at Camp Clarke, near Northport, on February 12, 1899

Average Annual Precipitation: 22 inches

Major Rivers: Big Blue, Elkhorn, Little Blue, Loup, Missouri, Niobrara, North Platte, Platte, Republican, South Platte

Major Lakes: Enders, Harlan County, Jeffrey, Johnson, McConaughy, Harry Strunk, Sutherland, Swanson

Trees: ash, basswood, box elder, cedar, cottonwood, elm, hackberry, locust, oak, pine, walnut, willow

Wild Plants: blue flag, buffalo grass, chokecherry, columbine, evening primrose, goldenrod, grama grass, larkspur, phlox, poppy, spiderwort, violet, wild plum, wild rose

Animals: badger, coyote, mule deer, muskrat, opossum, prairie dog, rabbit, raccoon, skunk, squirrel

Birds: bald eagle, cardinal, chickadee, duck, flicker, goose, heron, pheasant, plover, purple finch, quail, sandhill crane, woodpecker

Fish: bass, carp, catfish, crappie, perch, pike, trout

Endangered Animals: American burying beetle, black-footed ferret, Eskimo curlew, least tern, pallid sturgeon, Topeka shiner, whooping crane

Endangered Plants: blowout penstemon

Black-footed ferret

TIMELINE

Nebraska History

1500s Pawnee Indians migrate to what is now Nebraska from farther south

1682 Explorer René-Robert Cavelier, Sieur de La Salle, claims the lands drained by the Mississippi River for France. The region, known as the Louisiana Territory, includes Nebraska.

1700s Arapaho, Cheyenne, Omaha, Oto, Ponca, and Lakota Indians thrive in Nebraska

1739 Frenchmen Pierre and Paul Mallet become the first Europeans known to cross Nebraska

1762 Louisiana Territory is given to Spain

1800 Louisiana is given back to France

1803 The United States gains Nebraska with the Louisiana Purchase

1804 Explorers Meriwether Lewis and William Clark lead the U.S. government's first expedition through Nebraska

1819 The U.S. Army builds Fort Atkinson, its first post in Nebraska, to protect the frontier

1823 Fur traders found Bellevue, Nebraska's first town

1843 Large numbers of pioneers heading for the Far West begin traveling across Nebraska on the Oregon Trail

1854 Missouri, Oto, and Omaha Indians give up lands and move to reservations; Nebraska Territory opens to settlement

1863 Daniel Freeman is the first person in the nation to file a claim under the Homestead Act, settling in Beatrice, Nebraska

1865 The Union Pacific Railroad starts the first line west across the United States, heading out from Omaha

1867 Nebraska becomes the 37th state

1874–1877 Huge swarms of grasshoppers descend on Nebraska, destroying crops and causing many settlers to lose their farms

1892 Mathew O. Ricketts becomes the first black person to serve in the Nebraska legislature

1895–1900 Nebraska's Populist Party fights for agricultural reforms

1904 Congress passes the Kinkaid Homestead Act, which promotes settlement in the Sandhills and the Panhandle

1929 The Great Depression begins

1937 Nebraska's first unicameral legislature meets

1939 Oil is discovered in southeastern Nebraska, helping the state recover from the Great Depression

1942 Kingsley Dam is completed on the North Platte River, forming Lake McConaughy

1948 The Strategic Air Command sets up headquarters at Offutt Air Force Base, bringing thousands of jobs to Nebraska

1967 Nebraska votes to adopt a sales tax and an income tax

1968–1969 Race riots erupt in Omaha

1980s Many farms are sold and replaced by small industries, changing Nebraska's economy

1990 The state government passes a major tax increase to fund public education

1992 Nebraskans vote to adopt a state lottery

ECONOMY

Agricultural Products: beans, beef cattle, corn, grain sorghum, hay, hogs, oats, potatoes, soybeans, sugar beets, wheat

Sugar beets

Manufactured Products: chemicals, farm equipment, electrical equipment, food products, machinery, printed material, scientific instruments, transportation equipment

Natural Resources: limestone, petroleum, sand and gravel

Business and Trade: banking, insurance, real estate, tourism

CALENDAR OF CELEBRATIONS

Crane Watch Each spring more than 500,000 migrating sandhill and whooping cranes stop to feed near the Platte River on their way north. Two great places to spot them are Rowe Sanctuary and Fort Kearny.

Arbor Day Celebration Nebraska City goes all out for Arbor Day, the holiday founded by its resident J. Sterling Morton to encourage the planting of trees. The April festival includes a tree giveaway, hands-on craft demonstrations, and a parade.

Lady Vestey Victorian Festival Nebraska heroine Evelene Brodstone grew up in tiny Superior, traveled to China as secretary for the Vestey meatpacking business, then married the company boss, who was also an English lord. In May, her hometown remembers her with a 19th-century costume parade and a formal afternoon tea.

Nebraskaland Days Each June North Platte celebrates Nebraska's frontier spirit with a nine-day blowout featuring country music and dancing, barbecue, and the rough and ready Buffalo Bill Rodeo.

Omaha Summer Arts Festival Creativity is the theme of this June celebration. You can try your hand at painting or jewelry making, or even learn how to perform a magic show.

Nebraska's Big Rodeo Held each July in Burwell, this action-packed event features chuck-wagon races, steer wrestling, bull riding, and a longhorn cattle show.

Nebraska Czech Festival The polka bands at this August celebration in Wilber will have you dancing in no time. If your feet get tired, eat some kolache or check out the parades of Czech costumes.

Nebraska State Fair
Farmers from every county in the state show off crops and livestock at the end of the summer in Lincoln.

Nebraska State Fair

Kass Kounty King Korn Karnival Plattsmouth kicks off this September festival by crowning a local couple king and queen of "Kornland." The royal pair presides over ugly-pickup and slow-tractor contests, fireman water fights, and three big parades.

Old West Days Buckaroos from far and wide hit town for this three-day shindig in Valentine the first weekend in October. Festivities include a horse parade, cowboy poetry readings, old-time stage shows, and a Native American powwow.

Light of the World Pageant Since 1946, Minden has ushered in the holiday season with an outdoor Christmas pageant performed by local citizens. As thousands of onlookers brave the cold, the county courthouse flickers on in a display of 10,000 lights.

STATE STARS

Grover Cleveland Alexander (1887–1950) was one of the winningest pitchers in baseball history. Born in Elba, Alexander joined the major leagues in 1911 as a pitcher for the Philadelphia Phillies. After pitching a whopping 90 lifetime shutouts and winning 373 games, in 1938 he was elected to the Baseball Hall of Fame.

Fred Astaire (1899–1987) was a Hollywood dancer whose lighthearted elegance was world renowned. Born in Omaha, Astaire took dancing lessons at an early age and gave his first New York performance when he was seven. He later danced his way through dozens of movie musicals, including ten with his best-known partner, Ginger Rogers. *Top Hat* and *Swing Time* are among his many beloved films.

Fred Astaire

Max A. Baer (1909–1959), a native of Omaha, was a hard-hitting boxer who knocked out more than 50 opponents during his 12-year career. In 1934 Baer beat Italian bruiser Primo Carnera to become the heavyweight champion of the world. Baer might have kept his title longer, but he loved being in the spotlight more than he liked training. While clowning around in the ring, he lost to the less talented James Braddock in 1935.

Max A. Baer

Marlon Brando

Marlon Brando (1924–   ) is an actor who shot to stardom playing tough characters living in a harsh world. Brando got his start at the Community Playhouse in Omaha, the city where he was born. In 1947 he made a big impact on Broadway in the play *A Streetcar Named Desire*. He later turned to Hollywood, where his riveting performances in *On the Waterfront* and *The Godfather* brought him two Academy Awards.

William Jennings Bryan (1860–1925) was one of America's most brilliant public speakers. As a lawyer in Lincoln, he became active in the Populist revolt, a movement to make conditions better for farmers. Bryan ran for president three times and spoke out often for the rights of working people. He later was a prosecutor in the famous Scopes Monkey Trial, a court case in which a teacher named John Scopes was tried for teaching the theory of evolution.

William Jennings Bryan

Johnny Carson (1925–   ) was the longtime host of the television program *The Tonight Show*. Carson moved with his family to Norfolk when he was eight years old, and he studied speech and radio at the University of Nebraska. After working as a radio announcer in Omaha, he headed for Hollywood, where his appearance on America's favorite late-night talk show made him a household name.

Willa Cather (1873–1947) was a writer whose works paint a vivid picture of life on the western plains. Cather moved to Nebraska with her family when she was nine. While living in Webster County and Red Cloud, she fell in love with the prairie. She later captured its drama in such widely read novels as *My Antonia* and *O Pioneers!*

Buffalo Bill Cody (1846–1917), was a legendary cowboy entertainer. Cody settled the Nebraska Territory with his family when he was eight and became a Pony Express rider at age 14. After earning his nickname hunting buffalo, he traveled to New York, where he demonstrated his frontier skills on stage. Buffalo Bill's own extravagant Wild West shows, which started in Omaha in 1883, toured the United States and Europe for 30 years.

Buffalo Bill Cody

Crazy Horse (1842–1877) was a visionary Lakota leader whose bold resistance to the U.S. government made him a legend in his own time. Crazy Horse grew up hunting buffalo on the Nebraska plains. In 1876 in a fierce battle to defend Lakota freedom, he defeated General George Armstrong Custer at the Battle of the Little Bighorn. He was killed at Fort Robinson the following year.

Ruth Etting (1897–1978) was known in the 1920s and 1930s as America's Sweetheart of Song. Born in David City, she rose to fame in Chicago, where she met and married a gangster who managed her career. *Button Up Your Overcoat* and *Ten Cents a Dance* were among her most popular songs.

Ruth Etting

Edward Joseph Flanagan (1886–1948) founded Boys Town, a community where homeless and troubled children can live, work, and learn. A Catholic priest who was born in Ireland, Flanagan moved to Nebraska in 1912. He created an entire village for needy boys outside of Omaha, with its own chapel, post office, gymnasium, and school.

Henry Fonda (1905–1982), who was born in Grand Island and grew up in Omaha, was one of the most popular movie stars of the 1940s and 1950s. Fonda was shy as a boy, and it wasn't until he was 20 that he tried out for his first play. He eventually moved to Hollywood, where his quiet good looks propelled him to fame in such films as *The Grapes of Wrath* and *Twelve Angry Men*. At the end of his career, Fonda won an Academy Award for his performance in *On Golden Pond*.

Gerald R. Ford (1913–   ), a Republican from Omaha, served as president of the United States from 1974 to 1977. A U.S. congressman from Michigan for 25 years, Ford became vice president after Spiro T. Agnew resigned from office in 1973. When President Richard M. Nixon also resigned, Ford took his place, helping the nation recover after Nixon's presidency was tarnished by the Watergate political scandal.

Bob Gibson (1935–   ) was a baseball great whose pitching, batting, and fielding talents were unparalleled. During his childhood in Omaha, Gibson suffered from rickets and asthma, but that didn't stop him from playing ball. He joined the St. Louis Cardinals in 1959, and within a decade, he had chalked up 3,000 strikeouts, something only one other player had done before.

Bob Gibson

Joyce C. Hall (1891–1982), who grew up in David City and Norfolk, founded Hallmark Cards. At age 18, Hall launched a mail-order postcard business from his room at a YMCA. Five years later he opened a greeting card plant with his brothers, which grew into the megacompany Hallmark. In 1957 Hall received the Horatio Alger Award for working his way from rags to riches.

Susette La Flesche (1854–1903), a member of the Omaha tribe, was a teacher, writer, and public speaker who led a campaign for the rights of Native Americans. La Flesche was educated at white-run boarding schools, and she moved easily between the white and the Indian worlds. In 1879 she traveled the country speaking out on behalf of the Ponca tribe, who had been forced to leave their Nebraska lands.

John G. Neihardt (1881–1973) was an award-winning poet who found inspiration in the culture of Nebraska's Native Americans. Neihardt's best-known work, *Black Elk Speaks*, grew out of conversations he had with a Lakota elder. Neihardt lived in Bancroft and Cuming County.

Nick Nolte (1941–   ), who was born in Omaha, is a popular film and television actor. Nolte's first love was football, and he played college ball before discovering the stage. After starring in the television miniseries *Rich Man, Poor Man* in 1976, he became one of Hollywood's most sought-after leading men. Nolte won a Golden Globe Award in 1992 for his performance in *The Prince of Tides*.

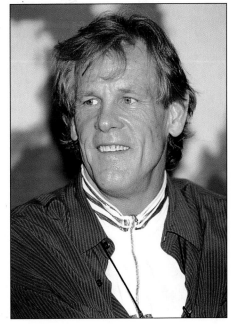

Nick Nolte

Tillie Olsen (1912–   ), a writer, was born and raised in Omaha. A child of the depression, Olsen never finished high school, and the responsibilities of work and family kept her from writing for many years. Today her short stories are widely read and admired for their emotional power. Olsen received an O. Henry Award for her story "Tell Me a Riddle," which was later made into an Academy Award–winning film.

Edwin E. Perkins (1889–1961) invented Kool-Aid. Perkins started concocting soft drinks at the age of 11 in Hendley, using a kit he ordered from a magazine. Soon he was running his own mail-order business, and the fruit-flavored beverage syrup he sold was much in demand. To cut shipping costs, in 1927 he converted the syrup to powder. Kool-Aid was an instant hit, and still is—more than 500 million gallons are consumed a year.

Mari Sandoz (1896–1966) was a writer known for her vivid descriptions of life on the Nebraska plains. Her many novels, histories, and biographies give an honest account of the violent conflicts that divided homesteaders, buffalo hunters, and Native Americans, as well as the joys they experienced in a beautiful land. Her best known work is *Old Jules*, a biography of her father.

Standing Bear (1829–1908), a leader of the Ponca tribe, launched a landmark protest to help his people regain their traditional lands. In 1876 the Ponca were forced to move from Nebraska to Oklahoma Territory, where more than a third of them died the first year. Standing Bear spoke out for the right to return to bury his son's remains, and in a groundbreaking court case, his voice was finally heard.

Malcolm X (1925–1965) was one of the most controversial figures of the civil rights era. The son of a black Baptist preacher living in Omaha, he saw racial injustice at an early age. He later found inspiration in the Nation of Islam, and gave passionate speeches against the evils of white power. Malcolm X was murdered in New York City in 1965.

Darryl Zanuck (1902–1979) was the producer of such classic films as *How Green Was My Valley* and *All About Eve* and cofounder of the company Twentieth Century-Fox. Zanuck started making movies in the 1920s, and in 1927 he produced the world's first talking picture, *The Jazz Singer*. Known as one of the most talented producers in show business, he later won three Oscars. Zanuck was born in Wahoo.

Darryl Zanuck

TOUR THE STATE

Chimney Rock National Historic Site (Bayard) This towering landmark on the Oregon Trail can be seen from 30 miles away. The visitor center tells of the many settlers who passed by it on their westward journey.

Joslyn Art Museum (Omaha) You can see some of the 19th century's most beautiful paintings in this world-class gallery. Built in 1931 with 38 different kinds of marble, the museum itself is a work of art.

Museum of Nebraska History (Lincoln) This three-story museum contains everything from moon rocks to a replica of a small-town Nebraska store.

Scotts Bluff National Monument (Gering) Visitors drive or climb to the top of this bluff for amazing views of the North Platte River valley and the Oregon Trail.

Buffalo Bill Ranch State Historical Park (North Platte) After touring cowboy legend Buffalo Bill's homestead, you can get in the saddle yourself for a trail ride around the grounds.

Buffalo Bill Ranch State Historical Park

Museum of the Fur Trade (Chadron) The first Europeans who came to Nebraska made a living trapping and trading in furs. Housed in an old post once owned by the American Fur Company, this museum sheds light on the lives of early frontiersmen and their Native American business partners.

Sidney Historic Downtown District (Sidney) Wild West legends like

Calamity Jane and Wild Bill Hickok used to pass through Sidney, a regular stop on the Union Pacific Railroad. A stroll downtown takes modern-day visitors past old-time shops, theaters, and saloons.

Stuhr Museum of the Prairie Pioneer (Grand Island) You can tour a blacksmith's shop, an old-fashioned railroad station, or a Pawnee Indian lodge at this huge indoor-outdoor museum.

Arbor Lodge State Historical Park and Arboretum (Nebraska City) The 52-room mansion in this park was once the home of Julius Sterling Morton, the founder of Arbor Day. Visitors can tour the lavish house and arboretum, featuring more than 250 kinds of trees.

Buffalo Gap National Grassland (Chadron) Prairie wildflowers burst into bloom each spring and summer among the wild grasses of northwestern Nebraska.

National Museum of Roller Skating (Lincoln) This one-of-a-kind museum traces the history of roller skating back to its beginnings in the early 1700s. Learn how sports like roller hockey, roller polo, and even roller basketball have changed with the evolution of the skate.

Fort Niobrara National Wildlife Refuge (Valentine) Nature trails wind through 19,000 acres populated with bison, elk, and more than 200 species of birds.

Nebraska National Forest (Brewster) In 1902, Nebraskans set out to increase its woodlands by planting trees in the Sandhills. They created the largest forest in the Western Hemisphere made by human hands.

Ashfall Fossil Beds State Historical Park (Royal) Around 10 million years ago, a volcanic eruption left the marshes of northern Nebraska buried in eight feet of ash. This incredible site offers a close-up view of the remains of hundreds of prehistoric creatures caught in the shower.

Carhenge and Car Art Reserve (Alliance) Created in 1987, this outdoor sculpture of half-buried cars is the spitting image of Stonehenge, a stone circle constructed in England in ancient times.

Harold Warp Pioneer Village (Minden) Old-time objects from antique tractors to china teacups are on display at this fascinating frontier museum. Its 28 historic buildings include a genuine Pony Express relay station, a one-room schoolhouse, and a sod house.

Museum of Nebraska Art (Kearney) This museum highlights artworks created in Nebraska, from the early days of exploration right up to the 21st century.

Fort Robinson State Park (Crawford) Visitors to Nebraska's largest state park can hike through pine forests, travel by stagecoach, and even sample buffalo stew. Its historic buildings recall the days when the U.S. Army clashed with Native Americans.

Agate Fossil Beds National Monument (Harrison) Thousands of fossils lie buried in this prehistoric graveyard. Trails will take you past those that have been uncovered—many still resting where they were found.

Girls and Boys Town (Omaha) Founded in 1917 as Boys Town, this historic home for troubled children now welcomes both boys and girls. Drop by and ask a student guide to show you around town.

Toadstool Geologic Park (Crawford) The sandstone in this section of the Oglala National Grassland has been eroded by wind and water to form weird, mushroomlike shapes.

FUN FACTS

The largest mammoth fossil ever discovered was found in 1922 near Wellfleet. Scientists believe this prehistoric beast was more than 13 feet tall.

The Union Pacific Railroad line between North Platte and Gibbon is the world's busiest stretch of rail for freight trains, with more than 130 trains passing through every 24 hours.

Roosevelt Park in Hebron boasts one of the world's largest swings. The seat has room for two dozen kids and is 32 feet long.

FIND OUT MORE

There's a lot more to learn about Nebraska. To get started, go online, visit your local library, or shop your favorite video or bookstore and look for these titles:

GENERAL STATE BOOKS

McNair, Sylvia. *Nebraska*. New York: Children's Press, 1999.

Thompson, Kathleen. *Nebraska*. Austin, TX: Raintree/Steck-Vaughn, 1996.

SPECIAL INTEREST BOOKS

Brown, Marion Marsh. *Susette La Flesche: Advocate for Native American Rights*. Chicago: Children's Press, 1992.

Conrad, Pam. *Prairie Visions: The Life and Times of Solomon Butcher*. New York: HarperCollins, 1991.

Ferris, Jeri. *Native American Doctor: The Story of Susan La Flesche Picotte*. Minneapolis, MN: Lerner Publications, 1991.

Myers, Walter Dean. *Malcolm X: By Any Means Necessary: A Biography*. New York: Scholastic, 1993.

Streissguth, Thomas. *Writer of the Plains: A Story about Willa Cather.* Minneapolis: Carolrhoda Books, 1997.

Warren, Andrea. *Pioneer Girl: Growing Up on the Prairie.* New York: Morrow Junior Books, 1998.

Wilkerson, J. L. *Scribe of the Great Plains: Mari Sandoz.* Kansas City, MO: Acorn Books, 1998.

Wills, Charles. *A Historical Album of Nebraska.* Brookfield, CT: Millbrook Press, 1994.

VIDEOS

Boys Town. Culver City, CA: MGM/UA Home Video, 1990.

The Chasers of Tornado Alley. Arlington, TX: Prairie Pictures, 1996.

WEBSITES

www.state.ne.us Official Nebraska website, full of tips, facts, and links.

www.omaha.lib.ne.us/transmiss/congress/omaha.html Listen to songs and chants of Omaha Indian elders, recorded more than a century ago.

www.nebraskahistory.org History site, with great links to pioneer diaries, photographs, and more.

INDEX

Page numbers for charts, graphs, and illustrations are in boldface.